WHAT PEOPLE ARE S

Psy-Complex in

One of my favourite challenges in *MasterChef: The Professionals* is when the contestants are presented with a wide array of leftovers (admittedly seriously generous, varied and upmarket ones) and asked to invent an exceptional plate of food in the usual ridiculous timescale. The results are generally much more impressive than you'd expect – real elegance, inventiveness and panache on a plate! This book is in much the same vein as those invention tests, woven from the best part of a lifetime's book reviewing into an extraordinary collection of intriguing, fascinating and inspirational texts. Each one is 'complete' in itself – an entertaining, informative and satisfying read; but brought together the collection offers so much more than the sum of its parts. It takes you on a rich and stimulating voyage into the 'psy' complex and (way) beyond – to give you insights and experiences far outside of what you may originally expect. Enjoy!

Wendy Stainton Rogers, Professor Emerita, Faculty of Welfare, Education & Health, the Open University, UK

This is an unusual book, drawing together reviews that Parker has written of other books. In each chapter, he offers us a model of the kind of critical engagement that turns a review into a dialogical contribution to debate, enlivening the works of others and bringing them into conversation. Taken as a whole, the book presents Parker's characteristic take on the psy-complex, developed across time through disciplinary crossings and collegial exchange across a wide international range of contexts, including Japan, South Africa, the US, Europe and the UK. It is a wonderful book to celebrate the 25th anniversary of the Discourse Unit and Ian Parker's unique voice and sustained contribution to rethinking the intellectual psy-terrain.

Professor Jill Bradbury, School of Human and Community Development, University of the Witwatersrand, South Africa.

Ian Parker takes us on a critical adventure through the dense undergrowth of the psy-complex exploring the perennial and important questions of psychology and psychoanalysis' relations to knowledge, ideology, social theory and political practice. This is an unusual book which positively invites the reader not only to think for themselves but to actively question the psy-profession's construction of the world.

Ron Roberts, author of *Psychology and Capitalism*, Zero Books, 2015.

Psy-Complex in Question

Critical Review in Psychology,
Psychoanalysis and Social Theory

Psy-Complex
in Question

Critical Review in Psychology,
Psychoanalysis and Social Theory

Ian Parker

Winchester, UK
Washington, USA

First published by Zero Books, 2018
Zero Books is an imprint of John Hunt Publishing Ltd., Laurel House, Station Approach,
Alresford, Hants, SO24 9JH, UK
office1@jhpbooks.net
www.johnhuntpublishing.com
www.zero-books.net

For distributor details and how to order please visit the 'Ordering' section on our website.

Text copyright: Ian Parker 2017

ISBN: 978 1 78535 749 7
978 1 78535 653 7 (ebook)
Library of Congress Control Number: 2016963053

A CIP catalogue record for this book is available from the British Library.

Design: Stuart Davies

Printed and bound by CPI Group (UK) Ltd, Croydon, CR0 4YY, UK

We operate a distinctive and ethical publishing philosophy in all
areas of our business, from our global network of authors to
production and worldwide distribution.

CONTENTS

Acknowledgements

This book brings together versions of review papers that were published in scattered places and are often inaccessible. Chapter 1 was published in 1992 as 'Review of K. Danziger (1990) *Constructing the Subject', Journal for the History of the Human Sciences*, 5 (1), pp. 111–14. Chapter 2 was published in 2008 as 'Review of D. Hook's *Foucault, Psychology and the Analytics of Power', Psychoanalysis, Culture and Society*, 13, pp. 217–220. Chapter 3 was published in 2012 as 'Review of Brown, SD and Stenner, P. (2009) *Psychology without Foundations: History, Philosophy and Psychosocial Theory', Subjectivity*, 5, pp. 464–467. Chapter 4 was published in 2012 as 'Postcolonial Psychology: Review of Richards, G. (2012) *'Race', Racism and Psychology: Towards a Reflexive History (2nd Edition)*, London and New York: Routledge and Hook, D. (2011) *A Critical Psychology of the Postcolonial: The Mind of Apartheid', Postcolonial Studies*, 15 (4), pp. 499–505. Chapter 5 was published in 2001 as 'Review of M. Terre Blanche and K. Durrheim (eds.) (1999) *Research in Practice: Applied Methods for the Social Sciences', PINS (Psychology in Society)*, 27, pp. 148–150. Chapter 6 was published in 2008 as 'Politics versus Psychotherapy' [review of Totton], *Psychotherapy and Politics International*, 6 (2), pp. 91–97. Chapter 7 was published in 1998 as 'Review of R. House and N. Totton (eds.) (1997) *Implausible Professions: Arguments for Pluralism and Autonomy', European Journal of Psychotherapy, Counselling and Health*, 1 (3), pp. 477–479. Chapter 8 was published in 2001 as 'Review Essay: On M. Billig (1999) *Freudian Repression: Conversation Creating the Unconscious', Journal of Community and Applied Social Psychology*, 11 (1), pp. 69–73. Chapter 9 was published in 2006 as 'Review of Manning (2005) *Freud and American Sociology', The Sociological Review*, 54 (2), pp. 384–386. Chapter 10 was published in 2012 as 'Review of Frosh's *Psychoanalysis Outside the Clinic: Interventions in*

Psychosocial Studies', *Subjectivity*, 5 (2), pp. 223–240. Chapter 11 was published in 2011 as 'Review of Birksted-Breen, D., Flanders, S. and Gibeault, A. (eds.) (2010) *Reading French Psychoanalysis* (London: Routledge)', *Psychodynamic Practice*, 17 (1), pp. 106–109. Chapter 12 was published in 2009 as 'Review of Dany-Robert Dufour's *The Art of Shrinking Heads: On the New Servitude of the Liberated in the Age of Total Capitalism'*, *British Journal of Sociology*, 60 (2), pp. 424–426. Chapter 13 was published in 2008 as 'Temptations of Pedagogery: Seventeen Lures (Review of J. Lacan's *The Other Side of Psychoanalysis: The Seminar of Jacques Lacan, Book XVII)'*, *Subjectivity*, 24, pp. 376–379. Chapter 14 was published in 1999 as 'Clinical Lacan: Review Essay on Bruce Fink's *A Clinical Introduction to Lacanian Psychoanalysis: Theory and Technique'*, *PS: Journal of the Universities Association for Psychoanalytic Studies*, 2 (2), pp. 69–74. Chapter 15 was published in 2005 as 'Review of Loose (2002) *The Subject of Addiction'*, *Theory & Psychology*, 15 (5), pp. 739–743. Chapter 16 was published in 2007 as 'Review of Ruth Golan's (2006) *Loving Psychoanalysis'*, *Psychodynamic Practice*, 13 (2), pp. 207–209. Chapter 17 was published in 2015 as 'Method in Madness: Review of P. Gherovici and M. Steinkoler's (2015) *Lacan on Madness: Madness, Yes You Can't'*, *Self & Society: An International Journal for Humanistic Psychology*, 43 (3), pp. 278–281. Chapter 18 was published in 2012 as 'An emptity signifier, not: Review of Stijn Vanheule's *The Subject of Psychosis: A Lacanian Perspective'*, *Psychoanalytical Notebooks*, 25, pp. 211–213. Chapter 19 was published in 2004 as 'Rakan no seishin-bunseki', *Journal for Lacanian Studies*, 2 (2), pp. 318–328. Chapter 20 was published in 2007 as 'Review of Yannis Stavrakakis (2007) *The Lacanian Left'*, *Situations: Project for the Radical Imagination*, 2 (2), pp. 117–121. Chapter 21 was published in 2010 as 'The sublime object of ideology', *Journal of Critical Psychology, Counselling and Psychotherapy*, 10 (2), pp. 109–110. Chapter 22 was published in 2007 as 'The Parallax Review: Review of Slavoj Žižek's (2006) *The Parallax View'*, *Ephemera:*

Theory & Politics in Organization, 7 (3), pp. 486–488. Chapter 23 was published in 2010 as 'Into God with Žižek and (Almost) Out Again': Review essay of A. Kotsko, *Žižek and Theology* (Continuum, London, 2008), M. Pound, *Theology, Psychoanalysis and Trauma* (SCM Press, London, 2007) and M. Pound, *Žižek: A (Very) Critical Introduction* (Eerdmans Publishing Co, Grand Rapids, MI, 2008), *Subjectivity*, 3pp, 122–124. Chapter 24 was published in 2007 as 'Jodi's Dream: Review of Jodi Dean's (2006) *Žižek's Politics'*, *Ephemera: Theory & Politics in Organization*, 7 (3), pp. 481–485; and Chapter 25 was published in 2011 as 'Lock Work: Review of Fabio Vighi's *On Žižek's Dialectics: Surplus, Subtraction, Sublimation'*, *New Formations*, 72, pp. 174–175.

I have modified some formulations in the published papers and excluded extraneous material. I have, however, included most of the material as it was originally published and reflect on shortcomings in the introduction to this book. I am, as ever, grateful to Erica Burman and my colleagues in the international network around the Discourse Unit for their critical comments and support during the preparation of this volume. The mistakes must surely in some way be theirs too.

Introduction

Review and Critique in the Psy-Complex

This book is about the psy-complex, it is also about how we might critically review the psy-complex, and it is about a key element of contemporary intellectual reproduction, the 'book review' as critical peer evaluation that sustains the academic community. You will learn more about the psy-complex from different vantage points as you go through the book. The reviews gathered here cover the domains of psychology, psychoanalysis and social theory, specifically the work of Jacques Lacan and Slavoj Žižek. You will see how a book review works, some good and bad examples.

I was trained first as a psychologist, but was 'critical' of the theories and methodologies used in the discipline from the beginning of my career, and then when I trained as a psychoanalyst, and started to use ideas from that tradition to critique psychology, it was already in the context of social-theoretical debates that connected research on subjectivity with cultural and political context. This book brings together books I have enjoyed reading and for which I was given sufficient journal space to elaborate some kind of argument with. You will see that I like to argue with a book in a review, and this gives a polemical edge to each of the pieces that makes them, I hope, more enjoyable to read and more likely to encourage you to go and read the books themselves.

In this introduction I will try to spell out what I do not do when I write a review as well as what I try to do (even if I do not always succeed). So, I will look at how the book review can operate as a genre for training psychologists who want to think critically about what they do, how the reviews gathered here illustrate the emerging shape of critical psychological argument and debate, and how psychoanalytic and social theory contributes to new ideas about human agency.

Reading and Arguing

A bad book review begins with an account of what the reviewer felt when they were first asked to read the book and what they thought the book might be about. The 'when I was asked to review this book' narrative takes a further more nightmarish turn when we are told what the cover looks like, and even what the cover blurbs written by friends of the author might have said about it. Then we can be pretty sure that we will be led into a 'the next chapter is about' structure which always seems to be proof positive that Lacan (1991/2007) was right when he claimed that language did not only serve as a medium for communication but also, and more importantly, served to deaden what it pretended to merely describe (as in Lacan's comment, borrowed from a reading of Hegel, that the word is the murder of the thing).

Yes, you can discover something about what the reviewer does and does not like from the way they approach a book, but the review itself should be treated as a text that is crafted to bring to light certain issues and, if it is being honest, shows us what it is trying to steer us away from. The way to do that crafting is to set up the parameters for the review at the outset so that the description of the content of the book is set against the background assumptions that will be mobilised in support of or against it. This way of establishing the ground rules could be thought of in the terms used by Billig (1999) when he points to the importance of thinking as taking place by way of 'argument', by way of a debate or dialogue with oneself and imagined audiences. When an argument is made in favour of one point of view, for example, we will be in a better position to understand what is going on and where the argument is leading if we have a clue as to what point of view is being argued against.

So, a review that simply tells us what the book is about avoids the key pedagogical opportunity of explaining why these or those issues are so important, and then, following up that explanation with reference to the book in question, showing how we are taken forward and what obstacles still remain in place. A book review is the public face of peer evaluation, and sometimes the review itself will have a format which is rather similar to the other more obscure gatekeeping procedures in the academic world. It is very different from cases where a reviewer of a research proposal needs to give their feedback within the rigid set of categories that have been laid down by the funding body, the worst of these being in the form of tick-boxes in which exchange between applicant and their colleagues becomes completely impossible. It is different from cases in which the intended publisher of a book proposal seems only interested in the sales potential and market for the product, about the extent to which the book simply repeats what we have read many times before but in brighter more appealing covers. And it is different from when the research application or book proposal is sent to the reviewer with the promise that the feedback will be confidential, that the reviewer will not have to argue their own position or be accountable for what they say because their identity is concealed.

The similarities become more apparent in open dialogical reviewing which some journals have been willing to experiment with in recent years (including some within the broad 'critical psychological' tradition). Then the reviewer is asked to give a narrative account through which they show they have understood what they have been asked to evaluate (even if this is refracted through the particular position they take, and they have often been asked to be the reviewer precisely because they come at things from another angle), identify the key points that are being argued for as the basis for the work and give an evaluation which weighs up the strengths and weaknesses. In fact, in the case of reviews of journal articles, a good editor will want the evaluation to include a degree of latitude so that they have the freedom to put the review in the balance with other reviewers' comments, and then the freedom to decide themselves if it is worth going ahead. And the polemical element of the review can sometimes be very useful in helping the editor gauge whether the article is going to provoke debate. (I know of cases where all the reviews of a journal article have been so hostile but, at the same time, so well-argued, that the editor was convinced that the thing should be published.) A book review should accentuate that polemical aspect so that the reader has some point of purchase on the book (even if the aim of the review is not only to get someone to purchase it), some way in which it enables them to keep a critical distance from it. As recent 'critical psychological' work has pointed out, the attempt to develop a psychology 'without foundations' actually means that argument from a variety of different competing theoretical perspectives becomes even more important (Brown and Stenner, 2009).

Disciplinary Contexts

There is a common confusion in the discipline of psychology over the question of 'reflexivity' and what it involves. Because most psychologists have bought into the idea that psychological research should be about individuals abstracted from social context, they tend to think that reflexivity should amount to an invitation to speak about where they are coming from and what they feel about the work they are doing. This is 'psychological reflexivity' and it entails the inclusion of what is sometimes called a 'reflexive analysis' subsection of the report in which the reader is told how fascinated the researcher was in this or that issue, and then even how difficult they found the process of carrying out and analysing the work. That is, we learn something about the writer but very little about how we might read and think critically about what they are describing. This psychological reflexivity is sometimes sold to students as an invitation

4

to write about their 'journey' into the research. What this then adds to our understanding of what went on as the research and the report was put together, apart from a little voyeuristic entertainment (which is why student researchers often still find this kind of reflexivity a bit creepy), is pretty close to zero. That kind of reflexivity would be a rather annoying distraction if it was to become part of a book review.

The other way of approaching reflexivity is what we find in good qualitative research which attends to the conditions in which the work was carried out and which then, necessarily, reflects on the consequences for how we treat psychology itself (Terre Blanche and Durrheim, 1999). This second way of approaching reflexivity requires us to map ourselves as researchers in relation to the conceptual assumptions that frame how we and others understand the questions that are asked and in relation to the institutions and professions that place limits on the way we can ask those questions (House and Totton, 1997). That is, we set out as clearly as we can the context in which we do our work, and so enable the reader to access the frames in which the questions appear and then are followed through or abandoned without explanation. This is one of the starting points for a good book review, that the review either spells out directly (if there is space), or at least sketches out along with a description of the book, the contours of the conceptual ground against which the book might be evaluated. Then the reader also has a chance to participate in the kind of assessment that the reviewer is aiming to carry out.

A review should take a critical distance from the book in question, and, as can be seen in some of the reviews in this book, that is a bit easier when another context that is possibly unfamiliar to the reader has to be described so that the account of the book in the review will then make some sense. This is necessary when the review is of a set of disciplinary debates that are quite outside the frame of taken-for-granted assumptions in the host discipline, of the particular uptake of psychoanalytic ideas in theology, say, that has to be explained to an audience of psychologists and social scientists (Kotsko, 2008; Pound, 2007, 2008). Sometimes this task is made more pressing because the book is addressing a cultural context that is different, and critical work in psychology has been able to learn many lessons from the way that understandings of and research into subjectivity varies so hugely across the world. While psychoanalysis is usually assumed by psychologists to be one thing – about Freud and post-Freudians as represented in the textbooks – it is clear, for example, that it actually takes quite different forms in different cultures, in France (Birksted-Breen, 2010), say, or Japan (Shingu, 2004), or Israel/Palestine (Golan, 2006).

Transdisciplinary Opportunities

A good review should have the shape of a little essay – it has a beginning (in which you are given some orientation to the issues at stake and some clues about where the reviewer is coming from), a middle (in which the logic of the argument of the book in question is traced out, and this logic of the argument may not exactly correspond to the sequence of the chapters, let alone the titles that the author of the book has given to their chapters), and an end (which might be an extended punchline thrown with the book at its intended target or thrown back at the book for failing to deliver on some of its promises). An essay review gives more space to follow this shape, and an essay review of two or three books gives even more scope for an elaboration of an argument rather than a simple repetition of what each of the books is ostensibly about.

This book focuses on issues in critical psychology, psychoanalysis and social theory respectively, but the boundaries between those categories are disturbed at different points. Psychologists have been compelled by force of argument by colleagues in other disciplines to look at how their assumptions about the human subject are 'constructed' rather than gathered as facts about behaviour and experience (Danziger, 1990). The pretence that psychologists might have something to offer by way of therapeutic expertise to help people, for example, is then questioned not only by psychoanalysts (Vanheule, 2011) and social theorists (Vighi, 2012), and those who work at the interface between psychoanalysis and social theory (Gherovici and Steinkoler, 2015), but also by psychotherapists themselves, some of whom are already ahead of the game in thinking through political consequences of analysis in practice (Totton, 2006). It then becomes clear that it is not possible to understand psychology itself without looking at how its stories about people are embedded in relations of power (Hook, 2007). Recognition of this leads us, as it has some 'critical psychologists', to reflection on the cultural-historical conditions in which we do our work in the 'West' and on the way psychology as a discipline has been implicated in colonial assumptions about our 'selves' and 'others' (Richards, 2012).

The turn to psychoanalysis operates for some psychologists as an escape route from the worst of the discipline (Hook, 2012), for Freudian and post-Freudian theory offers a quite different way of accounting for subjectivity which then often connects with political critique (Stavrakakis, 2007). When that turn to psychoanalysis occurs, which in some variants has led psychologists to break away from their own departments and forge a completely new domain known as 'psychosocial studies' (Frosh, 2010), there is still a concern with the relation between the 'individual' and the 'social'. That alternative psychoanalytic conception of the individual, however, does not treat the 'social' as a set of variables that can be patched on to the abstracted 'psychology' that the discipline has usually traded in. Instead, such taken-for-granted psychological topics like addiction are reconfigured so as to be almost unrecognisable to researchers in the old laboratory-experimental paradigm (Loose, 2002).

This then leads us to link what we have been trying to do inside psychology with 'social theory' that has itself been reenergised by psychoanalysis. This psychoanalysis is very different from the old normative psychoanalysis that deadened a couple of generations of psychologists, and sociologists for that matter (Manning, 2005). It is psychoanalysis that refuses to endorse treatment that aims at adaptation of the individual to society, which is what psychoanalysis became in the United States, and instead aims at a political exploration and subversion of the boundaries between normality and supposed abnormality (Dufour, 2008).

Psychoanalysis in Lacan's 'return to Freud', to take a case in point, has not always lived up to its radical pretensions, has had to negotiate its own way through US-American culture (Fink, 1999), but in the hands of social theorists like Slavoj Žižek (e.g., 2006) and his followers (e.g., Dean, 2006) it has drawn attention to the intimate connection between public ideology and private fantasy (and between private ideology and public fantasy). This most radical departure from the kind of work we have been used to inside the discipline of psychology can actually illuminate the most fundamental questions about the individual that we were told we should be solving (Žižek, 1989). So, you will learn what the emerging shape of critical argument and debate is around the psy-complex today, how psychoanalytic and social theory can contribute new ideas about human agency, and see how important the book review genre is for reflecting on and developing critique of the psy-complex.

Part I

On Psychology and Psychotherapy

1

Constructing the Subject

Danziger, K. (1990) *Constructing the Subject: Historical Origins of Psychological Research*. Cambridge: Cambridge University Press.

Kurt Danziger's book, which we can take to be about how to read the history of psychology, also necessarily raises issues as to how we should read the critical history he presents. The final chapter, 'The social construction of psychological knowledge', foregrounds a number of theoretical positions that the reader could mobilise to make sense of the material in the preceding ten chapters. The tensions between these theoretical positions are the source of both the weaknesses and the strengths in the book overall.

It is fitting to start this review with the author's glance back over his text, a text which is now intractably there as the condition for what can be said next; for the conceptual apparatus of psychology is a text of this type, and we can only glance back as subjects and objects of its gaze, positioned by the discourses of the discipline. Danziger argues that 'we have been examining the dependence of the knowledge product on the conditions of its production, and this has necessarily entailed a deconstruction of the generally false claims to universality that were commonly made on behalf of psychological knowledge' (p. 191). Accounts of the production of knowledge, the deconstruction of that knowledge, and a position of truth from which we could evaluate it are assumed here and back in the rest of the text.

Danziger presents, in chapter six, 'Identifying the subject in psychological research', a history of the constitution of the object of psychology (that object which experimenters, in a typically bizarre elision of human and machine, call the 'subject'), a history which is open to a Foucauldian recasting later on in the book but which mercifully does not, in the actual account, incant the terms 'observation', 'surveillance', 'calibration' and 'regulation' in every paragraph. It would perhaps have been appropriate, however, to extend the theoretical gloss on the history to show how the relationship between researcher and researched (and subject and object) became part of the conditions of possibility for the emergence of the 'psy-complex'. The 'psy-complex' is the set of institutions, practices and popular representations of psychology within which each member of the population is understood (and within which they understand themselves). The Foucauldian complement of Danziger's book here would be Rose's (1985) *The Psychological Complex*.

The meticulous tracing of the relationship between the theoretical architecture of our academic research sector of the psy-complex and the economic practices of professional investigation in chapters five, 'The triumph of the aggregate', and seven, 'Marketable methods', is an effective destruction of the truth claims of psychology, but whether this is a *deconstruction* is another matter. The use of the term 'deconstruction' has come to mean many things, and it is used often now as a synonym for 'critique'. But Danziger's use of the term a page after a fairly lucid account of Foucault's (1977) work raises the question of how we should undermine the privilege accorded to psychological expertise, and use, as leverage against that expertise, other subjugated forms of knowledge. When Danziger argues that psychology makes 'generally false claims' to universality, he quickly (too quickly, perhaps) turns to address critics of his position who might read this as an abandonment of any true knowledge and reassures them that interdisciplinary work should be able to sift through the history of psychology and rescue findings that could be treated as true. There is a brief appeal in earlier pages to Roy Bhaskar's (1989) realism, but the style of argument here is closer to the programme of German

'Critical Psychology' around Klaus Holzkamp (1992) (though shorn of Marxism).

Through most of the book the adjudication as to how material from psychology's past should be treated as true or false would seem to be for Danziger, in some form, a scientific question. Chapter three, 'Divergence of investigative practice: The repudiation of Wundt', for example, retells in detail the story of the ways in which Wundt, as a kind of sorcerer's apprentice, constructed a variety of laboratory experimentation by means of which he did not intend to investigate all mental processes, and which carefully demarcated forms of introspection not amenable to psychological investigation. Laboratory experimentation then became the fetish of followers (such as Titchener) whose work then distorted and consumed Wundt's own: 'Virtually everything that happened in modern psychology was a repudiation of Wundt, explicitly or implicitly' (p. 34). Elsewhere, however, the (explicitly 'false') positivism of most psychology is counterposed to (implicitly 'true') 'common sense'. The question which must be asked whenever the category of 'common sense' is appealed to, or counterposed to scientific knowledge, is 'whose common sense?' (For many white male middle-class psychologists, the discipline of psychology is their common sense.) Some varieties of common sense enjoy power over others, and a critical history of psychology needs to connect with those who suffer this power and the complex that buttresses it.

At the very end of the book, Danziger takes up the political nature of his history, and (quite rightly) explores the alliances that psychologists could make with those outside the discipline. This is a fraught question at present for social constructionist psychology, particularly in the United States, for it now seems clear that the success or failure of a critique of psychology rests not so much either on the internal coherence of the argument or on the probity of 'our' scientific community, as on the links between researchers 'inside' the discipline and those 'outside'.

Danziger carefully describes in chapter two, 'Historical roots of the psychological laboratory', the split between subject and object in scientific procedures which constituted Wundtian modern psychology, and he deals well in chapter eight, 'Investigative practice as professional product', with the construction of a community which takes certain procedures and 'facts' as given, and other ways of seeing as outside the domain of proper science. The question is, then, an 'alliance' with whom?

An instructive case in point here concerns the quite different reception of two different critical psychology texts in the public realm, and the reasons why there were those different receptions. Compare Carol Gilligan (1982) counterposing the (stereotypically masculine) 'objectivity' of positivist psychology to a feminist understanding of women's 'common' sense (the 'different voice') with Ken Gergen (1991) who counterposes the truth claims of modern 'sciences' such as psychology (which think they are arriving at the truth) to postmodern and fragmented forms of narrative (in which no social construction is 'true'). Gilligan gained the respect and support of many women inside and outside psychology, while Gergen has recently attracted some (very) negative public attention (e.g. *New York Times* Book Review, 23 June 1991). The issue is not so much that Gilligan replaced psychological truth with feminine truth and that Gergen will replace psychological truth with nothing, as an issue to do with the nature of the alliances that each account permits. Gilligan succeeded in producing an account which resonated with the experiences of women oppressed by the institutions of the psy-complex and made an effective alliance with them, while Gergen has succeeded in ruling out an appeal to the experience of any oppressed group 'outside' the discipline, and has thereby necessarily failed to make an alliance with anyone. Like most other histories of psychology, Danziger's is, by default, male (etc.), but he does pose the question as to who we write our histories for.

Constructing the Subject is a thorough account of the production of the science of mental life, a science which has succeeded in simultaneously sapping and feeding the forms of individuality that people in the dominant culture of the West experience themselves as possessing. At many points, through the rhetorical devices of cautious style, the use of figures and tables and standard photographs from the history of psychology, the text could be read as a standard history. At other points, when the connections with theoretical and historical perspectives are identified (albeit buried in the footnotes), the account touches a deconstructive dynamic and a radical social constructionism which really could, as Danziger hopes, reach out 'to groups of people who are more interested in psychological knowledge as a possible factor in their own emancipation than as a factor in their management and control of others' (p. 197).

2

Foucault, Psychology and the Analytics of Power

Hook, D. (2007) *Foucault, Psychology and the Analytics of Power.* Basingstoke: Palgrave Macmillan.

Psychology is a conceptual apparatus that now functions as one of the most important disciplinary mechanisms in contemporary neoliberal society. It provides and furnishes dominant models of the self in much of the English-speaking world, and it operates as a moral compass for how we should make sense of our behaviour, our thoughts and our sentiments. It is also one of the most powerful pretenders to scientific legitimation of psychotherapeutic practice, and so it is a force that professionals working in all fields of mental health have to reckon with. There have been many critiques over the years, but psychology has succeeded quite well so far in defending itself against various Marxist, feminist, humanist and psychoanalytic attempts to displace it from centre stage, to challenge its peculiar normalizing definitions of what health and happiness should be like. The resources psychology mobilises in response to these critiques – resources it often mobilises without even having to think about what it is doing – have been the focus of critical analytic work in the last 30 years, work that draws on the theory of Michel Foucault. Now Derek Hook has seized the baton and runs faster and further than other Foucauldians to date.

Foucault provides an invaluable alternative historical vocabulary, a counter-language and counter-memory, to tackle the way the discipline of psychology has become embedded in networks of practical-theoretical space, the 'psy-complex'. Those networks of power-knowledge at the one moment warrant the turn to the individual subject as target of programmes of social engineering. At the very same moment, apparatchiks in those networks call upon this particular discipline, psychology, to implement those programmes. The detailed analytic study undertaken by Foucault and a number of associated historians and social theorists begs a question as to how psychology could really continue when it has been dismantled by such critics so effectively, so many times.

It is necessary to remind ourselves that the survival of psychology in the face of these waves of critical work cannot only be put down to how it is intermeshed with other elements of the psy-complex and with even more deep-rooted ideological and state practices. The problem is twofold. Either Foucauldian work on psychology has tended to be elaborated in painstaking detail from outside the discipline, which makes it too easily discounted by those inside who pull down the shutters against the rabble and their representatives in sociology, who should not speak about what they do not understand. Or Foucault has been mixed and matched with a variety of deconstructive or so-called postmodern complaints inside the discipline, complaints that can then be dismissed as being but parts of a chorus of illegitimate political grievances.

Now, at last, in *Foucault, Psychology and the Analytics of Power*, Hook draws the reader into a sustained engagement with and deployment of Foucault's work that cuts from inside the belly of the beast. This book shows how psychology is embodied in the subjects upon whom the discipline works, and he shows how it is located in forms of space that must be configured as forms of power. At the same time he deals with those who have diluted Foucault's arguments on grounds of political expediency, and the book traces an ambitious arc of argumentation that dispatches along the way 'discursive' psychologists who reduce genealogy to the play of language. So, there is discussion of therapeutic constructions that treats them as disciplinary practices, and an analysis of embodiment that proceeds by 'desubstantializing' power. Historical analysis, which Hook demonstrates through a close reading of the construction of aberrant forms of sexuality, must take seriously Foucault's dictum that knowledge is not made for understanding but for cutting. The reference Foucault makes to 'heterotopia' (in lectures at the Collège de France in 1975–1976, published in 2003) is used to good effect to open up relations between power, knowledge and the organisation of space in gated community spaces in South Africa (from which many of the examples in the book are drawn). And then we are plunged back into the heart of psychology again in the final chapter with an examination of how affect might be retrieved by those working with Foucauldian ideas in the discipline.

So far, so good. There are, however, some points in this inspiring and energetic book where we have to be careful not to get swept along by the argument, and these actually turn around Hook's allegiance to Foucault. On the one hand, there is an attempt to remain faithful to his master, perhaps too faithful. On the other hand, there are some departures, and these departures are also quite problematic. So, for example, Hook too quickly endorses a particular reading of Foucault that loyally sides with him against Marxism and a class analysis. Does being faithful to Foucault really require such a sharp differentiation from Marx? There is a peculiar moment, for example, when we are told that Foucault shows us that power does not only function as a commodity, and this is linked to what is glossed as Foucault's 'wider critique of Marxist forms of thought' (p. 64). But this really is precisely where Foucault coincides with Marx, for their analyses of commodification under capitalism concern, among other things, how phenomena like power come to be understood, how they come to operate for each individual subject. Hook's representation of Marxism makes it seem complicit with capitalism, both concepts to be studiously avoided, of course. This line of argument is also unfortunately symptomatic of much contemporary Foucauldian scholarship, an ideological trend of work that is actually itself complicit with capitalism and hostile to political traditions on the left that still insist that another world is possible.

It is one of the conventional wisdoms of much Foucauldian work that even references to capitalism should be treated with suspicion, and while Foucault himself was often quite explicit about the connections between his work and the Marxist tradition, there is a danger now that refusal of all forms of power will simply fold into a refusal to take responsibility for the process of social change. Or, to put it more bluntly, that the social forces that can really challenge psychology and the psychologisation of politics – Marxism and feminism to name but two such social forces – will be blocked by those who see these political traditions as simply new manifestations of power knowledge.

And then, Hook takes another tack late in the book where he seems to want to take a distance from Foucault. There are intimations of this right back in the first chapter where there is a to-and-fro worrying about whether this line of work means dispensing with all of psychology or whether there might possibly be room for a little bit of it, the little that might be for good rather than bad. This good psychology could, perhaps, Hook suggests, draw on the work of Vygotsky, but he does not then show us how that particular framework might, as he puts it, 'fill in the blanks' (p. 61). By the last chapter, which is an impressive discussion of the place of affect in forms of governmentality, this possible good psychology has a new name, psychoanalysis. Here we are pulled into a puzzle about whether it might be possible to put psychoanalytic and Foucauldian analysis together. One of the advantages of Foucault's work is that it can be used to show the difference between psychoanalysis and psychology, and it would be irony indeed if Hook succeeded in conflating the two; at least, in a first move, running some kind of 'critical psychology' together with an avatar of psychoanalysis that then, necessarily, must betray psychoanalysis.

We could instead turn Foucault against Hook so that our Foucault becomes allied with Marxism, albeit in a tense uncertain relationship with it – and then it would be even more useful to interrogate forms of therapeutic practice like psychoanalysis, drawing attention to class dynamics that suffuse transference and interpretation. And we should then ensure that this Foucault never gives ground on the critique of psychology, and so is all the better able to resist the lure of what appears to be the reverse of psychology while it all the more insidiously inscribes it; that is, what now masquerades as psychoanalysis in 'scientific' evidence-based versions of treatment but simply does the work of psychology more efficiently because it is better attuned to the vagaries of neoliberalism. Debate on these issues – the opportunity to weigh up the arguments and find our way to a more tactical political reading of Foucault in and against psychology – is what Hook opens up in this marvellous book.

3

Psychology without Foundations

Brown, SD and Stenner, P. (2009) *Psychology without Foundations: History, Philosophy and Psychosocial Theory*. London: Sage.

The discipline of psychology, along with 'everyday psychology' that is sometimes counterposed to the discipline, operates through a complex mixture of rhetoric and practice. Its rhetoric lures us into the idea that the psychologists can see the phenomena they describe, and the practice circumscribes a place from which we speak about who we have become as psychological subjects. At the heart of psychology, then, is a paradox, which is that there is a claim to re-present what has been 'discovered' about behaviour, interaction, cognition or emotion but all this stuff has be represented, rhetorically framed in order for it to be intelligible. It is tempting to respond to disciplinary truth claims by pitting what we feel, and what we feel we know about ourselves against the psychologists, and many radical projects in and against psychology have come to grief as they try to play the apparatus at its own game. Against the appeal to experimental results is pitted an appeal to qualitative data, for example, and against the accounts of underlying emotion are pitted an account of actual affect. One cluster of 'foundations', the bad one we disagree with, is dismantled while another set is put in its place, and what we hope will be a more sophisticated rhetorical practice, built perhaps on incorrigible experience or unquestionable facts, starts off life as an alternative and then is easily recuperated, incorporated into the discipline itself.

Brown and Stenner's 'psychology without foundations' refuses to play this game, and circulates instead around the 'process of mediation' that constitutes what we take psychology to be. Each of the theorists – Artaud, Bergson, Deleuze, Foucault, Luhmann, Serres, Spinoza and Whitehead – explored in the book are put to work on a concept – embodiment, memory, subjectivity, life, communication, mediation, affect and process – to drive home the quasi-deconstructive lesson that any foundation can and should be unravelled in favour of process (which is, perhaps, why Whitehead is actually first in the series of theorists we encounter in the book).

Psychology is often a puzzle to academic researchers from adjacent disciplines because despite its attempt to keep the franchise on explorations of subjectivity, of the space of being that we have learnt in capitalist society to own as our 'individuality', the discipline does not seem to be able to adequately conceptualise its own subject matter. The problem is expressed in two ways. One expression of the problem is that certain figures – Piaget and Luria, for example – are written in to the history of the discipline as if they really were 'psychologists', and this itself entails some curious and misleading characterisations of their work in psychology textbooks. Others, like Holzkamp or Martín-Baró, are usually written out. What Brown and Stenner do in their book is bring some outliers from our history – William James is reclaimed along the way – and they make psychology take account of the work of other writers who have defined what subjectivity is in contemporary psychological culture (and they remind us that figures like Heidegger and Vološinov really need to be on the curriculum of an inclusive study of what it is to be a sentient subject today).

What they do not do so successfully is deal with the other expression of the problem of the franchise on subjectivity that the discipline of psychology protects, which is that debates inside the discipline are now not actually as rich in psychological content as debates outside in popular culture. One of the peculiar contradictions that mark this discipline now is that subjectivity as such is often evacuated from descriptions of behaviour and cognition. In this respect there is an intensification of the behaviourist project and modelling of cognitive processes on the kind of 'method' that most efficiently defined the discipline against neighbouring fields of study for many years. Meanwhile there is amazing expansion of talk about internal mental states saturated with affect which moralises about what it is to be a human being in the outside world. This flourishing of subjectivity outside psychology (of which a journal of this kind is symptomatic) takes quite particular forms that require careful examination, as has recently been undertaken, to take one key example, in the work of Jan De Vos (2011); there is a dialectical process at work in which a drive for certainty about the nature of pathology on the part of professionals and academics (those who seek foundations for psychology) is in tension with an incitement to plasticity and perpetual adaptation.

While capitalism in the late nineteenth and early twentieth centuries required a reduction of alienated life activity to measurable activity and insisted that the individual be respon-sible for themselves, neoliberal capitalism we enjoy and suffer today dissolves even more efficiently than ever all the putative foundations of our lives into air. Psychology, traditionally under-stood, now calls upon a form of 'anti-psychology' to extract surplus value from the workforce and enforce enthusiastic consumption of products and services. This means that the danger now is that the unravelling of foundations inside the discipline which Brown and Stenner accomplish so well could turn out to complement what is already being accomplished so much better in the outside world.

Perhaps it would be possible to say that this book is prefig-uring what life might be like beyond psychology and so beyond capitalism too, and in that case an attention to process would enable us to anticipate aspects of development that escape a linear and normative track laid down by psychologists for each individual segregated from the rest (Chakrabarti and Dhar, 2010).

But if that were the case we would surely need to strike a little more distance from the culture in which 'psychology' assumed importance, and we would need a little more deliberate engagement with the motif of 'ideology' that appears several times in the text as a rhetorical device.

What does it mean to say that something is 'ideological', and what are the stakes for the kind of argument that Brown and Stenner are making? A description in the book of a developmental psychology abstract shape video which privileged what was taken to be 'helping' over 'hindering' includes the comment that 'Presumably hindering is understood to be "anti-social" in the very particular ideological sense that it frustrates individual intentions' and then they note that what they call 'libertarian individualism' – the particular ideological view that is at stake here – 'is a very narrow view of social life... a historically and culturally specific world view' (Brown and Stenner, 2009, p. 87). This is all very well, and I have to say that I do also think that libertarian individualism is a narrow, historically and culturally specific world view, one that is indeed ideological. There are two theoretical glosses on what 'ideological' might mean in the book, so we are unclear whether it should be seen as helping or hindering us. First they quote with approval a claim that itself repeats the word in question to emphasise how an utterance depends not merely on the idea that speakers have of its meaning but to interlocutors' 'real, material appurtenance to one and the same segment of being'; that then 'gives this material commonness ideological expression and further ideological development' (ibid., p. 74). Later, however, they want us to sign up to an analysis that 'breaks with the notion of ideology and the corresponding idea of power as inherently repressive' (ibid., p. 188).

This conceptual ambiguity concerning the ideological crops up at other times when it seems to be evoked through various avatars (possibly because our authors are too queasy about the epistemological tangles an explicit use of the term would snare them in). It does look like references to 'the modern period' (ibid., pp. 14–15, for example) stand in for 'ideological' (the word is not actually used then, but the split between the 'subject' and 'matter' is presented at that point in the text as narrow, as historically and culturally specific). In the case of 'the empty abstraction of humanism' they spell out what is so bad about it but do not label it as ideological when they say that it is 'the self-contained, self-possessive model of the person whose mind is dominated by the faux-drama of petit bourgeois morality and intimacy' (ibid., p. 92). A humanistic psychological notion of 'self-actualisation' (in scare quotes in the text to alert us, perhaps, to it being something to beware of) relies on a 'bourgeois elitist platitude' (ibid., p. 181), and, over the page, we are warned against 'an illegitimate use of the conjunctive synthesis to "own" or become fixated on the name as though it had referred to some subjective attribute or essence' (ibid., p. 182). I like this, and it seems to me that when we chain together an 'illegitimate synthesis' with a 'bourgeois elitist platitude' and 'petit bourgeois morality' in the 'modern period' we must end up with something close enough to the way 'ideology' is deployed in Marxist theory, albeit a non-foundational form of Marxism (e.g., Bensaïd, 2002). Do not Brown and Stenner need this notion, and need to do a little more work to explicate it to make their critique cut sharper, and cut against the manifold kinds of oppression that contemporary neoliberal capitalism needs for it to run smoothly.

This book could not, of course, function as a new 'foundation' for psychology, and if it were to be used as a textbook for a critical course, care would need to be taken not to take any of the theorists favoured by Brown and Stenner as a 'model'. There is a danger that because these theorists articulate their own account of 'process' (or something close enough to process to be assimilated to the book's narrative) in such a convincing way, we might take the questions they raise as settled by them once and for all.

One way of taking the process of inquiry forward would be to invoke other theorists who might twist the narrative in some new directions. Perhaps 'Psychology without Foundations II' might comprise discussions of Abramović, Anderson, Barnes, Butler, Haraway, Lorde, Malabou and Spivak respectively (perhaps) on performance, representation, modernism, ethics, nature, culture, biology and colonialism.

4

A Critical Psychology of the Postcolonial: 'Race', Racism and Psychology

Hook, D. (2012) *A Critical Psychology of the Postcolonial: The Mind of Apartheid*. London and New York: Routledge.

Richards, G. (2012) *'Race', Racism and Psychology: Towards a Reflexive History (2nd Edition)*. London and New York: Routledge.

Psychology developed as a separate academic field of inquiry towards the end of the nineteenth century in Europe and became powerful as an academic and professional practice in the United States in the early twentieth century. US psychology was increasingly adopted as the benchmark for 'international' research in the discipline and, with some few exceptions, this kind of psychology – laboratory-experimental in form – had been rapidly globalised by the beginning of the twenty-first century. The time and place of its emergence, and phenomenal success today as its practitioners are called upon to advise, diagnose and improve the lives of individuals, raises a series of questions about its intertwinement with colonialism.

Graham Richards, in a classic text first published in 1997, now in this second edition of *'Race', Racism and Psychology: Towards a Reflexive History* includes discussion of postcolonial interventions, and makes a distinction between 'Psychology' (with a capital P) as the academic and professional discipline (and which is his main focus in the book) and the domain of 'psychology'. The book is part of a sustained project of, to borrow from the title of another of his books, 'putting psychology in its place' (Richards, 1996), that is, to locate this discipline at a particular point in history and simultaneously to, as it were, 'provincialise' the limited accounts of our internal mental states that are provided by psychologists. The second aspect, of 'psychology' (in lower case), refers to everyday forms of subjectivity which the discipline feeds upon to produce its own theories and then engorges with its own popularised 'findings' and speculations about human behaviour, cognition and feeling. This 'psychology' – itself colonised, we might say, by the discipline – is the main focus of Derek Hook's *A Critical Psychology of the Postcolonial: The Mind of Apartheid*, a theoretical articulation of the work of a range of anti-colonial writers.

The two books thus complement each other both in terms of their chronological account – Richards charts the background assumptions in the discipline as it gathered pace, and Hook brings us up to date with current debates and some suggestions as to how things should be taken forward – and in terms of the emphasis in critical research on the way our psychology is defined by psychologists and how we might reconfigure our inner states in defiance of what the discipline says about us.

Disciplinary conceptions of 'race' in psychology are, in Richards' account, the seedbed for forms of racism that granted a peculiarly virulent power to the discipline when European and then US scientists applied their work to colonial populations, and brought the results of that work to bear on different 'racial' groups at home. In one chapter, for example, Richards excavates a history of the 1898 Cambridge Torres Straits Expedition, which was to define how British psychologists thought about 'race', while another chapter provides a review of the way the 'race' and IQ debate has evolved from the late 1960s to the present-day. In both cases, we can see how different characters – intimately related to different political positions located in different class positions – took up contrasting views. At every point, the intersection of 'psychology' and 'Psychology' operates as a field of intense debate.

Richards' conceptual distinction between 'Psychology' and

'psychology', between discipline and experience, is useful but it is also one that Hook troubles, and the political-historical coordinates Hook uses are spelt out in his earlier work on the relevance of Foucault to critical work in the discipline (Hook, 2007). Within that Foucauldian frame, psychology is part of a constellation of theories and practices that have little in common bar the kind of methods they use to observe, measure and adapt individuals to the social (Rose, 1985). Psychology comes to operate during the late nineteenth and early twentieth century alongside psychiatry, social work and psychotherapy as part of the apparatus of the 'psy complex', and this psy complex requires that its subjects be willing and active participants.

This is a disciplinary matrix that calls upon individuals to speak to professionals, to bare their souls to them, and to speak to each other in such a way as to rehearse what we now recognise to be psychological ways of being. Now, the focus of Hook's intervention – the domain of subjectivity, how it is itself colonised and how it might be 'liberated' (to use a rather non-Foucauldian formulation) – takes centre stage. For without that 'psychology' among everyday folk that is drawing upon and then sustaining the work of the discipline, there would be barely any 'Psychology' as such.

It has been the hope of some 'critical psychologists' that the domain of 'psychology' might be reclaimed, and that the discipline of 'Psychology' could be turned into an empty shell, made irrelevant. And then, against this hope, there has been a nagging suspicion that, if the Foucauldian account is correct, everyday psychology is now the site of all of the disciplinary and confessional processes critical scholars wanted to avoid, and the psy complex is most of the time responding to the avid demands of thoroughly psychologised consumers. If this is right, then the truly dire history of the discipline that Richards describes pales into insignificance against contemporary neoliberal psychologisation which has succeeded in configuring us as victims of our own individual freedom (De Vos, 2012).

This is where the issues addressed in these two books directly connect with postcolonial debates, and where postcolonial theory becomes a valuable resource for addressing the history of 'race' and racism in psychology, in the discipline and in contemporary subjectivity. To shift psychology into the orbit of postcolonial studies is not merely to claim that the old history of colonialism (conceived as an instrumental mechanism for the production of new markets and for harvesting cheap labour power) has been ended and replaced by new forms of cultural dominance, as if we are now beyond colonialism as the exercise of brute force and living in times where ideological contest has become most important.

Richards shows very clearly that the early colonial period made use of psychology not only as a warrant for the exercise of Western expertise, all the more efficiently to subjugate populations and extract surplus value, but as a system of production of forms of self. The metaphors that clustered around 'race' produced the identities adopted by those who governed, and, crucially, also incited colonial subjects to understand themselves and thus to resist domination within the terms of those metaphors and practices (Mamdani, 2004). In this sense, the history of 'race' and racism was always already 'postcolonial', and ideological domination today is maintained within a matrix of coercion in which the production of identity is still necessarily accompanied by systemic violence (with Žižek (2008) the most obvious reference point here for Hook's overall argument).

Hook's study here again neatly dovetails with Richards', for his discussion of the place of the body – regulation of and resistance to racism as corporeal – shows us that the question of racism today is not simply an ideological one – pertaining to what traditional psychology would like to see as misjudged 'attitudes' and overly prescriptive 'stereotypes' – but operates at a deeper, more visceral level:

the (bodily, affective, pre-representational/prepropositional) aspects of racism in question may be 'extra-discursive' without being extra-symbolic. Such 'unmediated' forms of racism may, momentarily, elude the capture of discourse – at least in the sense of the network of systematic articulations that characterizes hegemonic discourse – without evading the broader context of symbolic functioning (Hook, 2011: 97).

The different sites from which Richards and Hook write also mean that their vantage points on 'race' and racism, colonialism and postcolonialism are, if not always complementary, usefully appreciative and questioning of each other. They have clearly had access to each others' draft manuscripts, and the overlap of material between the two books is crafted into the argument of each. Although Richards is based in Britain, and was once Director of the British Psychological Society's History of Psychology Centre, because the history of the discipline was so oriented to what happened in the US through the twentieth century, he is unravelling the discipline from within, from within one of the old colonial centres.

His attention to the role played by British imperialism and the way that colonial history was then articulated with the development of the discipline is designed to reinforce the argument that the rise of influence of US psychology was not necessarily a more malign alternative tradition. Rather, psychology formulated and researched in Britain went hand-in-glove with British colonial interests, and something similar played out as US psychology took up the baton, but with a difference. And the difference was that the US had a sizeable racially-oppressed population to deal with, both from the legacy of slavery and of mass immigration. Richards also shows how the continental European traditions of race psychology impacted upon Britain and the US. One might say that the role of Psychology as a discipline was to manage the transition from one form of Apartheid in the US to another, from that of explicit separate development and management of populations to that of toleration of difference as multicultural mask of power.

Hook, on the other hand, while also writing from inside Britain now, is oriented to South Africa, where he was educated, and to which he is still closely connected, including through the 'Apartheid Archive Project' which he returns to at different points in the book. The project has gathered accounts of life under Apartheid from South Africans in the then official 'racial' categories, and is now analysing them from different perspectives. In some respects, South Africa is a perfect laboratory in which to explore precisely the intersection between colonial and postcolonial rule. As a settler state built on the violent separation of populations it also elaborated anthropological, sociological and psychological justification for this separation. The very same conditions that led to the exclusion of the majority of the population from state power also, paradoxically, nurtured a subaltern intellectual tradition that tackled the dominant psychology with a resistant psychology.

This is work which includes what Richards glosses as 'Liberation Psychology', which is actually a rather misleading rubric which might lead some readers to imagine that this refers to action research perspectives in Latin America (Martín-Baró, 1994). This is not to say that there are not important challenges to the racism of Western psychology in the Latin American Liberation Psychology tradition, and these challenges could also be articulated with a parallel strand of 'Liberation Psychology' that aims to develop an 'indigenous psychology' in the Philippines (Enriquez, 1994). Richards' point is that inside South Africa itself during the Apartheid years, there was discussion of the work of Frantz Fanon (1967), the elaboration of a distinctive Black phenomenological tradition in the work of Chabani Manganyi (1973), and writings on 'Black Consciousness' by Steve Biko (1978) that had, as Hook shows, an explicitly 'psychological' dimension to them.

While Richards provides an excellent exhaustive historical survey of the attempts by White liberal academics in the US to understand and ameliorate the effects of racism, Hook explores already-existing 'postcolonial' refusal of the terms of debate set by the discipline of psychology and a connection with radical Black political action in South Africa.

The question as to what alternative psychology might take us forward is posed by Richards, but not pursued at any great length, and his concern is with the way that psychoanalysis as the great pretender to provide a more radical account of subjectivity actually replicates reactionary motifs of 'race' and racism even while it softens and interiorises these notions. That is, psycho-analysis questions the racism of those obsessed with race at the same time as pathologising those who rebel against it. Richards includes a fascinating discussion, for example, of John Dollard's 1937 *Class and Caste in a Southern Town*.

Dollard is now remembered by mainstream laboratory-exper-imental psychologists as a researcher into the 'frustration-aggression' hypothesis (a marrying of quasi-psychoanalytic hydraulic notions with a behaviourist account of the conditions which would trigger pent-up aggression toward certain social categories). Richards recovers a qualitative, non-experimental current of work in Dollard's study of life histories together with a balanced appeal against racial prejudice and against supersti-tious beliefs of 'Negros'. Psychoanalysis presents itself as an alternative Psychology and claims to access more directly the actual psychology of those afflicted by racism (both as perpe-trators and as victims), but Richards has an eye to how this alter-native is itself culturally-located:

The operation of these psychological mechanisms, notably those related to emotion, is comprehensible only within the complex socioeconomic context of Deep South plantation culture, with its fraught historical and cultural heritage. The binds in which the small emergent middle-class African American group find themselves are also dealt with at length. Behind all this lies the tension between the official American egalitarian ideology and the caste culture of the South in which the African American's under-caste position has to be sustained (Richards, 2012: 418).

There is an injunction here to historicise and culturally-locate forms of psychology, including psychoanalysis, that Hook is less keen on heeding. Taking his cue from Fanon, a psychiatrist who did indeed borrow psychoanalytic ideas to tackle colonial uses of psychoanalysis, Hook frames other non-psychoanalytic writers in South Africa in terms that are more explicitly psychoanalytic. This is where writers like Homi Bhabha are enrolled to press the shape of the argument. This is quite fruitful, and Hook provides a clear account of Bhabha's work, taking that work in some original directions which are grounded in the South African context (again drawing on accounts from the Apartheid Archive Project).

The category of 'enjoyment' is articulated with fantasy, and his argument accumulates a series of different psychoanalytic reference points, eventually bringing together elements of Fanon with elements of Žižek to explain exactly why the liberal balanced perspectives of psychologists (and most psychoanalysts) – the perspectives so neatly outlined and critiqued by Richards – will not work: 'Our failure to harmonize the paradigms of structure and experience (of imposed versus expressive phenomenology) points to an underlying deadlock, a traumatic and irreducible "irresolvability" within embodiment itself.' (Hook, 2011: 366).

This *aporetic* endpoint of the argument actually raises two questions. The first is the one posed by Richards as to the cultural specificity of psychological mechanisms of any kind. Fanon, for example, in his critique of Mannoni's (1964) attempt at an even-handed exploration of the 'inferiority complex' of the colonialist and the 'dependence complex' of the colonised, was clear that the forms of description he was providing – a phenomenology of humiliation and resentment overlaid with psychoanalytic vocabulary – was itself culturally and historically specific.

The second question concerns what is to be done when we have identified such a traumatic and irreducible deadlock. Richards does not have this problem because he has disposed of psychoanalysis as just one of a number of different ideologically-charged psychological models, and a reasoned scholarly response to this history will acknowledge the progress that has been achieved as well as their limitations. The 'reflexive' character of the argument, flagged in the title of Richards' book, means that we are able to understand how the discipline of Psychology is 'a product of the "psychologies" of those within it', and in times of colonialism this means that is necessarily racist (Richards, 2012: 418).

The implication of Hook's argument is that the non-rational grounding for forms of racism, particularly in the form of psychoanalysis he favours (that is, a quasi-Žižekian diametric alternative to the 'ego psychology' US tradition of Dollard and his like) must mean that a reasoned rational response is doomed to fail, destined to be caught in the irresolvable 'deadlock' he describes. It should mean that something beyond reason, some of the unconscious and fantasy should be brought to bear on challenging and changing racism, though he does not even hint at what this would be.

While the two books do present different perspectives that do, at many points, complement each other, we are left with 'deadlock' between them. This will either be resolved as the tides of history, assisted by the more liberal forms of postcolonial theory perhaps, gradually take us beyond the residues of the old colonial racism that Richards describes, or it will explode into new forms of crisis, a reorganisation of axes of power that also reconfigure what we think to be 'race' and really do take us into something genuinely 'postcolonial'. That might also entail, if we take Richards' route to change, a reflexive engagement with our everyday psychology and a break from what the discipline has told us about it so far, or it might require, if we follow Hook, the construction of a different theoretical standpoint that will give us some leverage against disciplinary *and* everyday psychology as we currently experience it.

5

Research in Practice

Terre Blanche, M. and Durrheim, K. (eds.) (1999) *Research in Practice: Applied Methods for the Social Sciences*. Cape Town: UCT Press.

This marvellous book performs a double subversion of 'methodology' for psychology students. First of all the book is a counterweight to the hegemony of US American psychology and its imitators in Europe. One of the little cracker quotes in the margin reminds us, for example, that the US Defence Department employs more psychologists than any other company or organisation in the world (p. 198). It is very difficult to find psychology textbooks that are not saturated with US American values and advertisements for particular culturally-specific kinds of psychology and psychopathology. *Research in Practice*, then, ensures that the usual US publisher's ruse, of binding in some extra pages about the part of the world it hopes to peddle its wares to, is thoroughly addressed. In this book we have hundreds of examples specifically about South Africa, ranging from the discussions of representation (of atlas projections of the world in which the size of Africa is diminished or emphasised) to arguments about how representations are made (of experiences of health among mineworkers in Carletonville). There is a deliberate localisation of research concerns, and so the concerns of South African students are hooked all the way through.

The second aspect of the subversion is the way that issues of representation and interpretation are unleashed from the domain of 'qualitative' research, and they come to pervade the whole text. Methodology is so crucial here because the discipline of psychology has been organised around methodological questions rather than substantive theoretical frameworks for most of its history. The question that has driven psychologists has been not so much how behaviour and mental process should be conceptualised but how they may be rendered visible. The neat divisions marked, as they usually are in methods books, by chapters about 'quantitative measurement' or 'interpretive methods' are dissolved in this book as each aspect of 'method' is made to meet the real world. The importance of contextualized practice is highlighted not only in discussions of participatory action research (which, as a margin note on p. 228 points out, 'is not a Euro-American import') or participatory rural appraisal (which permits theoretical issues of the 'epistemological function of distanciation' to be addressed, p. 404). It is also explicit in discussions of 'critical-emancipatory' approaches that are introduced in the context of 'programme evaluation' (which does not usually invite 'critical' study in psychology).

There is, however, a risk in presenting a text devoted to methodology in psychology, because precisely by playing into the answers that the discipline presupposes as the founding rationale for its existence – 'how should individuals be observed, measured and classified' – we might lose sight of the political stakes there are for psychologists when they avoid conceptual issues. Not only does 'methodolatry' (one of the 'common analytic errors' listed on p. 166, and quite rightly so) play a game by rules that critics need to be wary of, but it threatens to marginalise the role of *theoretical* reflection on what the game is about.

There are odd parts of the book which do seem to sideline theory, and perhaps the fact that the book is 'edited' rather than smoothed into one seemingly coherent text is an advantage here. Otherwise the idea of 'cleaning the data' described on p. 101 would throw a disturbing Harvey Keitel shape shadow from *Pulp Fiction* over the rest of the book. So, when 'grounded theory' is adduced as a framework to 'induce themes' (p. 141), this sits uneasily with the warning that a 'common analytic error' is simply to describe themes (p. 168). In fact, theory as such tends to be effaced in favour of 'method', and it is not enough simply to gesture toward the ideal of 'balancing' the two (as on pp. 404–405). Rather curiously, 'theoretical approaches' are discussed in most detail where they are glossed as 'standpoint method-ologies' in chapter 23 (and if the book really is so radical, why would it be necessary to hive off 'Marxist, feminist and black scholarship perspectives' into their own chapter?).

There are some pedagogical devices in the book that may backfire. The invitation to the reader to say what 'paradigm' they subscribe to could have the effect of *fixing* the reader rather than opening up possibilities for them and shifting them from the place they think they are (or the very idea that they should subscribe to one place or one identity at all). The injunction to consider the 'costing' of research (p. 57) also binds the reader into a certain kind of research enterprise, and this is left unexamined in other chapters in the book. Sometimes things are not as they seem, as when Tallis is quoted on p. 149 as if he is subscribing to a social constructionist perspective, when he is actually attacking that perspective (he refers to the 'vast inverted pyramid of discourse' as 'poised on the tiny apex of experience' precisely to privilege experience and to discredit those who only gaze at the 'pyramid'). And is not the 'logocentrism' described on p. 155 an always already *mediated* access to the world through the 'logos' or 'word' (and as such eminently deconstructable) rather than the emblem of immediate presence?

The book also asks a lot of a student reader on occasions, as when they are asked to 'design a website' on p. 187 (which is a task that surely requires some reflection on the way different modes of representation construct their objects in ways that require theoretical scrutiny), and when they are asked 'how does this picture make you feel?' on p. 295 but then left to it without any guide as to how they might work up that account, or reflect on it, or draw out lessons for how readings of pictures might be made. Cross-referencing from chapter to chapter sometimes does the trick (and in this last case it would have been easy to point the reader back to the semiotic studies elsewhere in the book).

Back to that double subversion that *Research in Practice* performs. First, the book is rooted in the South African context. But something more interesting is also going on. For at the very moment that a range of different methodological frameworks are teased out, explained and explored in the real world, the book becomes an instrument that is not at all only of use to South African researchers. This book will have an appeal to any researcher in the real world *anywhere in the world* who has been reflecting critically on what on earth the value is of ostensibly dull things like 'research design', 'programme evaluation' or 'multivariate date analysis'. The referencing of Internet resources – ranging from the TRC materials listed on p. 154 to help with postmodern theory signalled on p. 474 – means that the book is also an accessible meaningful guide for a student with a computer wherever they are. If UCT press gets its marketing right this book could find an audience in the US among critical researchers, and I know already there are psychology students in Europe who will be learning something about their own contexts by reading about these examples from what seem at first sight to be so far away.

Secondly, the book dissolves distinctions between method-ological traditions – 'quantitative' and 'statistical' measures versus 'interpretive' and 'social constructionist' explorations – that have bedevilled psychology, but it does so by making all this psychological stuff work in the broader domain of the *social sciences*. I have laboured 'psychology' in this review partly because I am writing for a psychology journal. But what 'psychology' actually is needs to be subject to question. And *Research in Practice* puts psychology on the spot by making us see action and experience in the world and how we might examine it as the priority so that the rather parochial concerns of the 'psychologists' with what they think the individual is can become a topic rather than an unexplicated assumption.

In sum, the book lays the ground for *critical* reflection on the discipline of psychology rather than mere methodology alone, and on more ground in the world than at first would appear to be the case. The introductory lists of aims for each chapter, the exercises and the boxes all make this an all the more enjoyable book to read. The contributors to the different chapters are, on occasion, identified by photographs where it will enable the reader to engage further with the particular kinds of work they are describing.

6

The Politics of Psychotherapy

Totton, N. (ed.) (2006) *The Politics of Psychotherapy: New Perspectives*. Buckingham: Open University Press.

The world of psychotherapeutic politics meshes all too well with my own personal predisposition to split and squabble, only to be able to define a position by way of what it is against. There are at least two ways to play this game, which this review paper explores.

One way would be to trace the sources of my reflex sectarianism to its real roots, to how the political domain is currently constituted. Then we have another twist to that problem, which is that bizarre as many organised political movements are, therapy training institutions often seem to trump them all. As Andrew Samuels points out in an excellent manifesto summary of his standpoint on the relationship between politics and the couch, 'therapists are completely crazy in their own professional politics and the way they organize themselves radiates that craziness' (p. 11). At a time when governments around the world are trying to regulate psychotherapy – a process, it should be remembered, that will squeeze out any space to discuss the issues aired in this book – it is a dismal task to persuade anyone that we can be trusted to regulate ourselves. Nick Totton provides a good overview of 'fragmentation, dishonesty, authoritarianism and rivalry' in psychotherapy organisations and makes some perceptive comments on the attempt by some to arrogate to themselves the right to say who is and who is not suitable, contrasting such hierarchical power ploys with networks aiming for 'a new model of accountability and organization' (p. 119). We also have a window into this crazy world in Petruska Clarkson's account of how 'ethics' in registration bodies is turned upside down, and it is indeed against that backdrop that practitioners of 'moral psycho-education' on the confessional television shows who reach an audience of millions seem to be the most 'observably and demonstrably helping people' (p. 106). The antics of those leading the main therapy training groups which function as a feeding ground of petty rivalries and demands for love must have the governmental regulators rubbing their hands with glee.

The little extra toxic twist to the problem – the transmission and condensation of political craziness into the heart of the profession that pretends to have something to say about forms of self-sabotaging misery – is signalled by Samuels' acute observation that the most ruthlessly successful politicians 'now couch their utterances in the language of the emotions' (p. 6). We need to explore further the consequences of this transformation in politics, for it draws attention to how the very tools that psychotherapists have used to understand politics have now been recuperated. The language of the emotions, which psychotherapists often imagine that they are experts in decoding and reformatting, has been absorbed, stripped of any challenge to power and turned against those who believed that another world was possible.

This poses a very difficult question for those wanting to use psychotherapeutic frameworks to tackle political issues, for now the stuff of therapy has already worked its way into social phenomena. It is not only that complex emotional dynamics drive conflicts around the world but that the language of the emotions is part of the apparatus that is used to incite and manipulate those involved. We can see this at work in various examples of progressive psychotherapeutic interventions, and there are clearly both attempts to mobilise concepts that will resonate with participants and, at the same time, attempts to outflank and outwit the forces that already make use of those therapeutic concepts.

Arlene Audergon and Lane Arye insist, in their account of work with a mixed group of Serbs, Croats and Muslims, that they must 'discover and support the group's innate wisdom, timing and direction' (p. 137), and such a strategy flows naturally from their belief that therapeutic change – therapeutic change as political change – must presuppose an underlying potential for 'deep democracy'. Such an appeal to 'democracy' as a primordial progressive bedrock for ecological, feminist and left politics is made by many of the contributors to the book. But at the same time, the notion of 'community' is now freighted with an ideological weight in which identification and cohesion often mix in a poisonous rather than curative therapeutic cocktail of justifications and practices. The effect is twofold; for at the same time as each of the communities in Croatia, for example, seeks collective accountability and responsibility, so governmental bodies aiming to stabilise the country under the new dispensation – neoliberal capitalism as opposed to the old regime of bureaucratic state-management – also call upon 'a deeper unity'. This means that Audergon and Arye must try to sidestep such already therapeutic conceptions of community unity and depth, and so they also attend to 'marginalized voices' (p. 136).

The difficult political question is whether it is really the 'margins of group life' that become the touchstone for political change or whether this is but a means to an end, to reach 'underlying shared human experience' (p. 136). Emanuel Berman quite rightly calls on analysts 'to confront openly major issues in their country's history', and opens up some wounds within the Israeli body politic, but this is then set in a context that works, again, in a twofold manner that has profound implications for how 'community' is to be understood. On the one hand, there is a focus on trauma among Israeli soldiers, and here we are told that 'as psychologists we have unique expertise, which is relevant to interpreting political processes as well' (p. 153). On the other hand, the divisions between 'some European professors' (those calling for an academic boycott) and 'Israeli protestors' (those searching for 'Israeli-Arab dialogue') are portrayed as harmful, leading to a feeling among some Israeli therapists 'of being backstabbed by their foreign colleagues' (p. 147). Once again, even though it is not explicitly named using the same vocabulary, we face a choice between seeing marginal voices as a force for change or dissension as a danger to the deep democracy to come.

Canny politicians seem to know now that while appeals to democracy can serve well enough in their rhetorical armoury, it is much more effective to draw on a discourse of 'accountability' and 'inclusion', and this is where the language of the emotions turns into the language of power, where the regulation of therapy meets political strategies of therapeutic regulation. The stakes are then raised for those trying to do progressive work in therapeutic settings, for the questioning of 'simplistic narratives' about the nature of society that radicals have always provoked now becomes a liability; as Jocelyn Chaplin notes, 'this very questioning has made possible the victory of consumer capitalism in which psychotherapy has fitted all too comfortably' (p. 159). Her account of the 'Bridge Project' in London exemplifies the dilemmas that radical psychotherapy faces, and it does so, again, in prioritising one particular dimension, gender, and its apparently seamless fit with the Department of Health. Documents prepared by government departments that call for 'transparency' and urge a 'partnership way of working and a reduction in hierarchy' require those who apply for funding to mirror the new language of the emotions in the service of the state, to speak the same language. The gap between tactics and ethics opens up when the therapeutic discourse – and here it is therapeutic discourse factored through feminism that is most salient – discourse that has already been recruited by the state feeds back and seeps into what the therapists say they are doing. This is striking, for example, in the claim that we would in other contexts read as an indictment of therapy that this mental health project 'is already working in ways recommended by the government with its theoretical commitments to equality' (p. 160).

The Bridge Project is well known among left, feminist and anti-racist therapy activists in the UK precisely because it has historically had a commitment to the intermeshing of dimensions of class, gender and culture in personal and political oppression. As with the contributions by Audergon and Arye and by Berman which show how the politics of community (whether coded through motifs of 'culture', 'ethnicity', 'race' or 'religion') separated off from other dimensions of oppression is then susceptible to being reworked within a conservative therapeutic language of the emotions, so Chaplin's account shows how the politics of gender disconnected from a broader political analysis become vulnerable to recuperation by politicians who are keen to speak our language as long as we also agree to speak theirs.

The role of class is addressed in the chapter on social activism by therapists in the US after 9/11. Katie Gentile and Susan Gutwill are quite upfront about tensions and choices, and perhaps it was easier to make this an explicit theme in a narrative account of activities by therapists seeking to reflect upon and intervene in debates following the terrorist attacks in 2001. Here (in the last chapter of the book) the contradictions are neatly displaced from the debate between psychotherapy and politics to differences within the emerging political groups formed by the psychotherapists themselves. That is, we can start to see how therapy in the realm of the political has also had to engage in a language which is not its own. Here the references to class served to divide the left from the liberals, but it is clear that the issue of class does itself already disturb liberal psychotherapists who find it difficult, though not, unfortunately, impossible, to render class into something that can be treated in the same way as other axes of 'difference', culture, gender, sexual orientation and so on, and as if those axes of difference can also be treated in the same way, as the names for a generalised 'otherism' Totton claims to have detected as including 'polarizing our own position as *against* any particular form of bigotry' (p. 35). As Gentile and Gutwill point out, it is one of the underlying assumptions of liberal practitioners that US society is a classless society with equal opportunity for all (and it is much easier to tackle various axes of difference in the consulting room if you think that different categories of person have had equal opportunity to get in there to start with). You cannot get very far in radical political work with therapists unless you tackle this ideological assumption and the nature of the system that cynically draws on neutralised therapeutic discourse to sustain itself, a culture 'which has a particular disdain for the unconscious, the unknown and the uncontrollable' (p. 175).

A first task for those working at the intersection of politics and psychotherapy, then, is, as Totton points out in his introduction to the book, to acknowledge and attest that all psychotherapists always already have a political view of their work: 'all psychotherapy rests on a theory – explicit or implicit, conscious or unconscious – of *how people should be*' (p. xiv). This book is so useful because it puts that argument on the agenda and then follows it through in a number of different contributions in which we, as psychotherapists, can begin to argue openly about what our political views of our work in the world are.

I learned very quickly when entering the strange reduced world of psychology and psychotherapy that we do need to take seriously the other way of playing the game of psychotherapeutic politics – the diametric opposite of that taken by our dear comrades in the struggle who write off our work as indulging emotional incontinence – and that is to search within myself for the peculiar psychological satisfaction that is obtained by engaging in political activity.

Now, we have to include in this kind of reflection some of the vantage points on the relationship between politics and psychotherapy that are advanced in this book, for there is an asymmetry in the relationship as it is staged here that should in itself ring some alarm bells. Lenin is reputed to have said of the debate between Christianity and Marxism that if it is a Christian engaging in the discussion then it is has progressive dynamic, but if it is a Marxist then this meeting of minds is necessarily reactionary. This is not so much an issue about who is more vulnerable, though a therapeutic framing might highlight the way the more defensive Marxist who refuses to acknowledge the spiritual dimension to existence is secretly yearning for something and so is the more vulnerable partner in the debate. Rather, it is an issue to do with institutional framing, in which there are few good theoretical resources to understand, from the standpoint of politics, how therapy works, and many more resources to understand, from the standpoint of therapy, how politics works. This book rehearses many of the motifs that have been accumulated over the years within the psychotherapeutic literature, by therapists wanting to connect with politics who in the process frame politics according to their own preoccupations. In this particular case we have to tackle both how psychological concepts are explicitly employed by different contributors to interpret and intervene in politics and to tackle how psychological concepts are implicitly used to make sense of the relationship between therapy and politics.

In a number of cases the reduction of politics to psychological factors is quite explicit, and there will be many practitioners who will find in this kind of reduction some comfort. It is even quite possible that a radical political position could be elaborated that draws upon the supposed knowledge that we have about human and evolutionary psychology that would serve to undermine some still dominant ideological nostrums about people, of 'how people should be'.

John Lees and Dawn Freshwater, for example, are quite clear

that they are concerned with a psychological understanding of alienation that should not be confused with a Marxist understanding of the term; then 'the mutual cycle of alienation' in therapy driven by specialised expertise 'results in devaluing the direct experience of clients and underrating their capacity to see experience as it is' (p. 129). This approach does at least, even as it introduces a phenomenological assumption – that we could ever be able to 'see experience as it is' – still leave open the way for another (Marxist) account of alienation to be brought in to the argument to provide a broader political frame for what is going on. Hilary Prentice and Mary-Jayne Rust likewise make an explicit ecopsychological claim about the meaning of nature to human beings that serves to unravel some of the culturally-specific notions about what meanings are immediately and obviously available for interpretation in psychotherapy; they describe, for example, the interpretation of the story of cutting down of a tree in childhood as reduced to the role of the father, and 'never about the tree in its own right' (p. 48). Again, there is an opening to another interpretation, other than concerning the father, that we are invited to think about even if we do not want to follow the idea that there is any such thing as a thing 'in its own right'. Judy Ryde also makes the useful and conveniently overlooked argument that psychotherapy is itself 'a western phenomenon' (p. 75).

There are tensions between contributions over the extent to which psychological phenomena could be taken on good coin and cashed out as part of a radical project for psychotherapy. For example, Sandra Bloom makes an impassioned case for the role of 'trauma' as a master concept which will underpin her analysis of a range of different social processes, and she then counterposes to this a 'natural democratic process' that would obtain in 'a calm, healthy, well-functioning system' (p. 24). Chess Denman, on the other hand, gives a concise overview of dominant and alternative views of sexuality, gender and object choice which sets itself against such prescriptions for what is taken to be normal or not, including sex in the consulting room: 'Depathologising even very aesthetically disgusting or morally reprehensible sex is a necessary preliminary to understanding it' (p. 66).

Let us turn to some of the more implicit psychological claims that are used not only to warrant psychotherapeutic practice but then also to think about how psychotherapy connects with politics. One of the ways to tackle the tension between psychotherapy and politics is to search for some kind of 'balance', nicely formulated by Samuels as the need 'to balance attempts to understand the secret politics of the inner world of emotional, personal and family experiences with the secret psychology of pressing outer world matters such as leadership, the economy, environmentalism, nationalism and war' (p. 4). As with the motif of 'democracy', which is something many of us in this context (and especially among these contributors) would be loath to admit that we did not unconditionally value and love with all our being, the motif of 'balance' is something that is valued as an unquestionably good thing by many in the book. This 'balance' between the two sides of the equation – psychotherapy and politics – then becomes the keynote claim in Totton's introduction to the book where it is refigured as 'mutuality': *Psychotherapy and politics each problematize the other, and each contribute to solving problems that the other faces.* (p. xvii).

But what if we were to go beyond these taken-for-granted categories 'psychotherapy' and 'politics' and see them as having been constituted as ineluctably antagonistic domains of practice? These domains of practice are reconstituted each time in a psychotherapy session in which two individuals separated from others, and separated from each other, meet to speak in a necessarily asymmetrical encounter, and they are reconstituted in each and every appeal to the language of the emotions by politicians who seek to anchor a particular programme of social management in the felt experience of their subjects.

It could be that the very attempt to connect psychotherapy and politics will serve to blur the difference between the two domains of practice, will run the two domains together so that contemporary psychologised politics – that style of management most appropriate to neoliberal government of deregulated services, a flexible competitive workforce and bespoke consumer markets – will seek a deeper warrant for its existence in psychotherapy. Psychotherapists then risk endorsing that kind of political system at the very moment they break out of their consulting rooms and becoming more socially engaged. In that sense the politics of psychotherapy has already been framed, and it is only the *separation* of the two that will allow psychotherapists, at least, to develop spaces in which we can take a critical distance from ideology, from any attempt to define how people should be.

7

Implausible Professions

House, R. and Totton, N. (eds.) (1997) *Implausible Professions: Arguments for Pluralism and Autonomy in Psychotherapy and Counselling*. Ross-on-Wye: PCCS.

This collection addresses issues at the heart of contemporary counselling and psychotherapy in a European context. House and Totton bring together professionals who are profoundly disturbed by the activities of colleagues who have ambitions to administer how we should help others in distress, and in particular enthusiasts for the drive for registration of therapeutic provision and training through bodies like the BAC and UKCP. The contributors are following in the tracks of Mowbray's (1995) comprehensive attack on the recent bureaucratisation of therapy and his careful debunking of the argument that if UK therapists do not regulate themselves they will fall prey to European Community regulations which would be far worse. The spectre of Europe is thus raised to frighten counsellors and therapists, and in the process the variety of different therapeutic approaches across the continent is obscured.

While Mowbray (who is also a contributor to this book) succeeded in showing that the 'protection' of clients in the UK registration process often amounted to little more than a protection racket for the professionals who had succeeded in jumping first into the relevant regulatory committees, House and Totton take the argument a good deal further. As they acknowledge in their introduction, to be 'against' registration in its current form entails being 'for' something else, and so the book had to include an elaboration of underlying assumptions about the nature of therapeutic work. This brings the reader to a series of profound reflections on counselling and psychotherapy as *moral-political* activities.

The first part of the book traces through the way professionalisation operates to inhibit and sabotage creativity, both for the therapist and client. The notion of 'transference', for example, is shown (in a chapter by John Heron) to operate as a warrant for the infantilisation of the client and aggrandisement of the therapist. Richard House picks up the bureaucratisation of therapeutic work in a deft critique of 'audit-mindedness' in a later chapter, and we thus get a sense of the psychic stakes of the registration process as something deeply anti-therapeutic. Both Heron and House follow through some of these ideas in later chapters.

Part two of the book ranges over issues of therapeutic 'expertise' (a myth nicely dismantled by Katharine Mair) and the 'models' some therapists are unwise enough to appeal to when they want to seem as if they could be experts (and the idea that there could be a 'core' theoretical model to underpin this expertise is helpfully unravelled by Colin Feltham). The third part of the book explores some of the costs of 'professionalism', and the chapters here range from personal accounts of the attempt to gain accreditation (for example, in the chapter by Sue Hatfield and Cal Cannon) to critical reflection on the whole enterprise of therapy (for example, in David Smail's exasperated complaint about the separation between therapists with their 'comforting illusions' and the real world).

A charge often made against the critics of registration is that they have nothing to put in its place, and we often hear insinuations that these kinds of people don't really have the best wishes of the clients at heart. However, this book does not evade the question of accountability. Rather, the approach the contributors take is very different from those who seem to think that 'ethics' can be added in through the regulation of training, or that accountability will magically appear in accrediting bodies that are accountable to nobody. A distinct version of therapeutic work is being appealed to here which puts ethics at its centre.

The fourth part of the book reviews some conceptual resources for the regulation of therapists, and here there are some interesting reflections by Andrew Samuels and Peter Lomas (both from within a broadly psychodynamic orientation). This is taken further in the fifth, final part of the book which includes some detailed suggestions for the practice of 'self-regulation'. There are more personal stories, and these are neatly complemented by an account (by Nick Totton) of the attempt by the Independent Practitioners Network to develop a new model of training, supervision and accountability.

There is an underlying agenda in this book, and this is where the ethical stance of the contributors is thrown into relief. Just as Mowbray's (1995) book was addressed, as his subtitle acknowledged, to the 'human potential movement', so 'pluralism and autonomy' in the subtitle of this book signals a distinctive view of what therapy is about. A picture of the therapeutic enterprise emerges from the book which is rooted in a *humanistic* view of distress and change. The worst and best of this approach is present in the book. On the negative side, there are certainly some serious lapses into psychic reductionism, and some chapters assume the existence of unconscious 'projection' and 'collusion' which would make a psychoanalyst blush (for example in David Wasdell's piece on the dynamics of accreditation). We are told many times in different chapters that the author feels that they have been true to themselves, as if that were sufficient for us to take their account on good coin. We do not hear the voices of clients who pay good money and sometimes exorbitant fees for the pleasure of being told what to do (or, in the most humanistic of therapies, being told to trust themselves).

However, on the positive side, the concern with openness about therapeutic stances and histories of training is a challenge to mystifying models of therapy which routinely legitimize deception and dissimulation. Humanistic approaches to therapy which revolve around the ability of clients to 'choose' are followed through here in models of accountability which make that process of choosing something tangible, and a model for good practice.

House and Totton bring together many voices against the regulation of a kind of work that surely should have as one of its foundational aims the provision of a space for varieties of experience that escape the constraints of our administered world. The arguments collected here are invaluable for the development of that kind of work. Each disdainful dismissal of Mowbray's arguments against registration and each avoidance of House and Totton's pleas for pluralism is a symptom of the state of an increasingly bureaucratised 'profession'. A careful reading of this book would serve to open up questions about registration and help therapists and clients register their dissent and find some better ways forward.

Part II

On Psychoanalysis and with Lacan

8

Freudian Repression

Billig, M. (1999) *Freudian Repression: Conversation Creating the Unconscious*. Cambridge: Cambridge University Press.

This book presents an argument for approaches to language which offer conceptual and methodological tools that can be brought to bear on psychoanalysis, specifically on Freud's writing, with 'repression' as a key motif but touching on many more besides. And Freud is also rescued from the malign grip of psychologists who misread him and psychoanalysts who render him only as someone as dogmatic and normative as mainstream psychology. At points in the book it seems as if psychoanalysis itself is being retrieved as a tradition that can be reread so that we can now creatively rewrite it and ourselves with it.

Billig admires the creativity of everyday argumentative rhetoric, and his recent writing has been devoted to a celebration of the 'witcraft' of ordinary folk as well as to a detailed description of the skills that much contemporary 'depopulated' psychology seems unable to do justice to. Psychoanalysis has always been present in his work, at least from his 1976 first book *Social Psychology and Intergroup Relations*, which included extended discussion of Freudian and post-Freudian views of group identity as well as their mutation in frustration-aggression theories in social psychology. His empirical studies of present-day fascism in *Fascists: A Social Psychological View of the National Front* in 1978 and later conceptual work on ideology in *Ideology and Social Psychology* in 1982 included critical reflection and reformulations of work on authoritarianism from within the Frankfurt School tradition. An important theme there was the way psychoanalytic theory was adapted and distorted to conform to the imperatives of US American culture. Now he explicitly returns to psychoanalysis after a detour through studies of rhetoric and discursive psychology, and so he brings something new to read Freud with. The studies of rhetoric in *Arguing and Thinking* (which first appeared in 1987 and then as a second edition in 1996) showed how things were opened up and made public. However, Billig now admits that his work there displayed 'a theoretical one-sidedness' (p. 51) and so this book *Freudian Repression* shows how things are closed down and made secret. Freud showed it already, and Billig shows us how Freud showed it, and what Freud closed down to show us it in the way he, Freud, wanted to.

The secret here lies in the little words and how we might observe what work they do. This is the human face of conversation analysis. This book is, among other things, an eminently accessible introduction to contemporary approaches to the study of everyday talk. They are approaches that can often appear arid and banal, and conversation analysis sometimes fits all too neatly into the most trivial empiricism that psychologists so often trade in. But Billig knows how to take dull things we usually take for granted, overlook as the commonplaces of a culture, and shine them up so that we notice them and appreciate what they do. There is a lovely example of this in the book where one of the favourite conversational-analytic devices of the 'adjacency pair' (used to specify how responses in conversational turns follow modes of address such as greetings or questions) is illustrated through a little window into Freud's ordered life. Freud pointing silently with his fork at an empty chair at lunchtime, Martha's explanation for the absence of his daughter Anna, and his nod of acknowledgement are opened out and elaborated in a way that the phrase 'two overlapping adjacency pairs' (p. 87) cannot on its own adequately define. In this example, Freud himself becomes the focus as a 'case' and, as with the other famous Freudian case studies analysed in the book, we learn not only that all the big stuff is in the little things (a lesson that all forms of discursive psychology take seriously) but that the little things only make sense if we are able to embed these mundane activities in the wider culture.

Billig's reading of the case of 'Dora' takes the argument further, and he uses the case to draw attention to the pervasive anti-Semitism that Freud seemed less than interested in as a contextual structuring feature of Jewish existence in *fin de siècle* Vienna. Dora and Freud were both to end their lives as refugees fleeing Nazism, and already their respective careers as hysteric and psychoanalyst were circumscribed and patterned by anti-Semitism such that this industrialist, Philip Bauer, would take his daughter to be sorted out by this doctor, Freud. And what they avoid speaking about in the fleeting comments about Christmas that pass between the two of them is homed in on by Billig so the comments might serve to speak of that which they cannot. Billig here picks up an argument from feminism and endorses it so that he can open up other questions in Freud's writing that have been carefully closed down: 'psychoanalytic writers themselves, including Freud, often created a forgetfulness: as the personal unconscious is remembered, so politics is forgotten' (p. 223). We could say that Billig is also in these examples 'repopulating' conversation analysis, doing justice to the unceasing repair work carried out by human beings as they try to make contact with others through the medium of language.

The task of 'repopulating' psychoanalytic case studies is also addressed along the way through a careful discussion of how the pseudonyms which are routinely and unthinkingly applied to Freud's analysands already frame them as characters marked by certain kinds of preoccupation and pathology. In some cases the substitution of 'Dora' or 'Elizabeth' for the real names of these young women is not immediately problematic. (Even here, though, the singular female name 'Dora' serves to individualise a problem and locate it in the victim, Ida Bauer, in a way that another term for the problem, say 'the Bauer case' which might include attention to the machinations of father Philip in the family, might not so readily.) In other cases it is important to remember the living human being beneath the label; psychoanalytic shorthand may serve to emphasise the role of rats or wolves in a patient's internal world at the expense of all of the other things in the world they faced. *Freudian Repression* demands both that the predicaments of real human beings are made present in forms of creative argumentation and the cultural processes that govern people's lives are made present in an account of ideology.

A certain ideological stance will always, of course, be betrayed by how one chooses to repopulate texts, and Billig's admiration for Freud makes him a little partisan here. We are invited to speculate about the perplexing inconsistencies between accounts of a case study, for example, by imagining Freud sitting late at night filling in the gaps (p. 62), and we are treated to letters from Freud to Martha, his betrothed, which already display something of a psychoanalytic as well as bourgeois sensibility to the subtle play of 'unpleasure' and civilization (p. 213). At times Billig repopulates his text a little too much with Freud at the expense of Martha; the fork pointing vignette could usefully be contextualized by patterns of patriarchy and studied boorishness by the male head of the household, better perhaps than suggesting that this is actually the kind of behaviour Martha would have been content with herself – would recognise these 'codes of politeness' (p. 87) – and moreover quite understandable because Freud was having a break from 'a hard morning's listening' (p. 90) to people on the couch downstairs. Here at least the ideological implications of the analysis are already present for us as readers to contest. The text is thoughtfully constructed so that the steps in the argument are clearly laid out, as well as some alternative tracks we might take in relation to it; it is a superbly clear text, open to disagreement. It is clear throughout the book that a moral-political stance governs the interlacing of textual examination and polemic, what Billig himself chooses to treat and how he frames it. The book is a passionate case for a style of analysis that combines the rigour of conversation analysis with the hermeneutic sensitivity of rhetorical psychology, and he adds to that analysis a cultural-political dimension that is too often studiously avoided by its practitioners.

In Billig's hands the analysis of conversation, discourse and rhetoric turns into a variety of critical psychology that is inspiring in its scope and style. This book is not only a compelling introduction to conversation analysis and the study of everyday strategies of argumentation as always already culturally and historically contextualized, then, it is also a splendid introduction to psychoanalysis. Not only does it bring Freudian theory to life, it also brings a scholarly eye to psychoanalytic understanding of Freud's work. For example, there is a close reading of the encounter between Freud and Ernst Lanzer, who was immortalised as the 'Rat Man' by later psychoanalysts. Billig prefers to call him 'Paul' (he argues that this is in order to be consistent with choice of names for other cases in the 'Standard Edition' of Freud's psychoanalytic writings), and he draws upon the 'process notes' for the case. The process notes are the first raw record the analyst makes of a case, usually session by session, as soon as possible after a meeting. Not only are the partial process notes from the *Standard Edition* scrutinized by Billig, he also draws upon the complete process notes for the case which have been published so far only in French and German. Subtle rewording of Freud's record of what transpired in the different versions are signs of the distinctive 'Freudian repression' that Billig wants to display.

Ernst Lanzer, in Billig's reading, is able to say 'but' as a 'defensive formula', but he is unable to follow this 'but' with something that would successfully direct attention away from what he really wants to avoid (p. 61). Billig's reframing of 'Paul's' problem does not only pertain to the patient, but also to what

Freud is doing when he accounts for what his patient is doing. Billig points out that Freud's case history is able to direct our attention away from aspects of the case he does not want to focus upon – the actual activity that his patient engages in to ward off unpleasant ideas – precisely because it directs our attention somewhere else, towards the cause that Freud has already identified. Freud succeeds where Ernst Lanzer does not. This analysis exemplifies a key argument running through the book about the nature of 'repression'; that is, that the 'discursive approach, if stretched a little, can provide the basis for under-standing repression' (p. 39), and repression is thus recast as part of the routine work of opening up and closing down topics that is necessary for polite talk to occur. A close examination of the way Mr and Mrs Graf instruct their son Herbert (who is the 'Little Hans' who suffers a father jealous of the attention his wife bestows on their son, a father who is keen to employ psychoana-lytic interpretation as a weapon to bring the family into line). Hans is instructed in how to avoid being 'rude', and by the same token to learn what rudeness is in this cultural context. This is the setting for a claim as grand as psychoanalytic claims but much more reasonable; that 'dialogic repression is universal' (p. 140). It is a claim that is much more reasonable than psychoanalysis.

At some points Billig himself is a tougher analyst than his hero, notwithstanding his modest measure of himself as but a child in comparison to the giant Freud in the last all too brief chapter on 'ideological implications' of the book (p. 253). Unlike Freud, he will not let slip by a pause in Dora's faltering account of why she stood admiring a painting of the Madonna. Billig comes across as a little reproving, and his disapproval of Dora as a young Jewish woman being transfixed by, identifying with, a Christian icon is at least as harsh as Freud's insistence that she should speak about who she loves: 'If she has obtained such complete gratification – if she sees the image as so blameless and morally superior – why cannot she say so?' (p. 245).

Psychoanalytic moralising about sexuality is displaced by, replaced with an attention to cultural identity and themes of ethnic betrayal. We could take this as one index of a key move that Billig makes in other parts of the book, from an argument for an analysis that might complement Freud to an argument against psychoanalysis (and so for something better, of course). As we might expect if we have taken Billig seriously, the move is present in the little words.

A case in point is the way the word 'however' operates in Billig's consideration of feminist criticisms of Freud's handling of 'Dora' (that he overlooked the behaviour of her father who had brought her to Freud to be put right): 'There is much that can be said to support such a general picture. However, something crucial is being omitted' (p. 221). Billig then goes on to flesh out what is routinely missing from psychoanalytic accounts of the case (and from feminist critiques of it), which is the constitution of Sigmund Freud and the Bauers as racialized as well as gendered subjects, that is as subject to anti-Semitism and as 'repressing' their Jewish identity in their talk (and in Freud's writing about the talk). The bulk of this chapter of the book works quite well with an interpretation of 'however' as having the sense of 'and', but Dora's identification with the Madonna is the cue for something else. Billig glosses Freud's own phrase for the image of the Madonna at the time, 'a favourite counter-idea', in a way that adds a slightly different sense so that it is now as if it is being treated by Freud in the case as 'a socially acceptable image' (p. 242). Psychoanalytically speaking, of course, something that is a favourite counter-idea is not at all the same as a socially acceptable image, quite the opposite. Now Billig switches to an account which invites us to remember his 'however' as a 'but', and despite his own reference to the key psychoanalytic concept of 'overdetermination' as meaning that 'one set of connections does not rule out others' (pp. 247–248) he now seems to counterpose his own analysis to other analyses which may focus on sexuality (as Freud's did, incompletely) or gender (as feminist readings do, incompletely).

Perhaps there is a logic, a form of dialogic repression demanded by our use of language, which demands this kind of counterposition. After all, as Billig shows in his analysis of the 'Rat Man' case, the patient 'Paul' is unable to do what Freud can do because he lacks the skill to follow his 'but' with something else. It is necessary that something else 'replace' what is to be avoided, and when something is expressed something else will be 'repressed'. Perhaps the slip from 'and' to 'but', and the consequent 'repression' of the possibilities that 'and' can still offer to our understanding, is of a piece with this dialogical process. But, and this is a big but, such a logic of dialogical counterposition itself calls for a different kind of psychology than that suggested by psychoanalysis. We might imagine a cognitive analytic therapist, perhaps one savvy with Bakhtin, diagnosing the way that all Paul does 'is to indicate discontinuity – to signal a dialogical move *away* without a replacement topic *towards*' (p. 64), and they may then develop a dialogical training package which would bring Paul up to speed on 'witcraft'. This certainly looks like an understanding of the problem which is compatible with the way a psychologist would understand it, but it also starts to look a little different from the way a psychoanalyst would see things.

So, is this book for or against psychoanalysis, is it psychoanalytic Freudian repression or repression of Freudian psychoanalysis? Perhaps things should not be posed in that stark way, but Billig does manage his relation to psychoanalysis in that way in the course of the book; at one moment presenting something which adds to our understanding of Freud, at another moment contrasting his reading with that of Freud. At some points in the book, then, it seems as if Billig is doing something quite different to psychoanalysis. This is where the conversation analysis kicks in and picks up turn-by-turn aspects of sense making that psychoanalysis fails to attend to.

At other points in the book it seems as if Billig wants to develop a genuinely Freudian argument, something that would be in the spirit of psychoanalysis and as a contribution to psychoanalytic theory. *Freudian Repression* is, indeed, a book that should be read by psychoanalysts, for it brings an argument to bear on the key texts; it illuminates and enlivens them. It is a project that deserves to be taken further, but it may be that some of the theoretical alliances Billig has made in this book and some of the resources he refuses to acknowledge need to be looked at carefully, and then need to be 'repressed' and 'expressed' respectively.

The key task that Billig sets out to accomplish is to shift psychoanalysis from the biologically based account that is present in many of Freud's own writings to a discursively saturated account. As Billig comments, 'Probably the biggest difference between the present notion of dialogic repression and Freud's original concept concerns the relations between psychology and biology' (p. 253). What follows from this? Rather than appeal to inherited dispositions to account for why we experience Oedipal conflicts with our parents or to wired-in stages of development to explain why some parts of our bodies become 'rude' when we grow up, we need to unravel how particular forms of language constitute particular forms of subjectivity. This is not at all to say that internalised mental processes in each individual could then be read off from general cultural tropes, but that the shared and singular development of consciousness, and what is avoided each time consciousness is displayed and remade, should be understood as discursively constituted. This sounds familiar, of course. It is uncannily close to the attempts by so-called 'post-structuralist' theorists of subjectivity in literary theory and then critical psychology to 'change the subject'.

Billig actually does the job better as far as the conceptual groundwork in Freud's own writing is concerned. Varieties of discourse analysis in psychology informed by post-structuralist theory were fine for tackling the discursive constitution of subjectivity in the matrices of power/knowledge and the psy-complex. Billig knows this, but makes it clear that this is not a route he wants to retread. There are even signs he wants to avoid those theoretical reference points. So, for example, when he argues that nowadays we are expected to talk about sex rather than keep away from the topic (p. 255) a reference to Foucault is conspicuous by its absence; Foucault, as an historian and theorist of the role of psychoanalysis as a form of confession, is actually shut out of the book altogether. However, Billig is also avoiding something, or rather someone else. He knows he is and precisely because of that he is able to weave his way through the book around what he wants to avoid all the more effectively. Billig says early on – and why not, after all 'anticipation' is viewed as a mature defence by mainstream US American ego psychology – that he 'did not want the book to develop into a running battle with Lacan' (p. 6). Later he declares that 'both the style and theoretical position of Lacanian psychology are avoided here' (p. 82). Would that things were that simply settled. Perhaps, paradoxically (and perhaps dialectically rather than merely dialogically), 'style' and 'theoretical position' indicate something of the distance and proximity that Billig stands in with respect to psychoanalysis and Lacan.

Perhaps the question of style does indicate something about Lacan, but perhaps Lacan's style conveys something that is necessarily psychoanalytic *as well as* something of his 'intellectual arrogance' (p. 7). Billig seems worried when an argument in the book 'seems to be slipping gently off the path of reasonableness' (p. 141), and it is certainly one of the virtues of *Freudian Repression* most of the time that it steers itself between 'bluff reasonableness' (p. 142) and the path of reasonableness, avoiding at all costs a style which is 'convoluted', as Lacan's undoubtedly is (p. 7). The problem is that psychoanalysis is not really reasonable at all. It is profoundly unreasonable, and it stares into horrible bizarre thoughts that quite outstrip what might be covered by the term 'rudeness'. When Billig makes repression into a dialogical process which pushes away what is 'rude' he confines the scope of what is actually constituted and shut away as the price of speaking to what 'the path of reasonableness' can encompass. He accuses Lacanians of having reached 'the grotesque extreme' (p. 36) of style, but perhaps it is not possible to elaborate an account which in any way reaches what is most grotesque and extreme about human thinking, understood discursively here still, without pushing out beyond the limits that language draws around what we are permitted to speak and think. Perhaps it is only an insistence on what is grotesque and extreme that will keep us close to psychoanalysis.

In this respect, then, Billig's own account is quite distant from psychoanalysis, and it is not so surprising to find him claiming at one point in the book that it is necessary 'to draw upon concepts and empirical findings from modern psychological research' (p. 142). After a step away from psychology into studies of rhetoric he steps into psychoanalysis, but psychoanalysis is not a psychology and Billig has taken a step back here, back into the discipline he so lucidly questions elsewhere.

As far as 'theoretical position' is concerned, Billig is actually closer to Lacan than he first appears. Lacan would seem to be, for many readers, an obvious reference point for a discursive under-standing of subjectivity in place of a psychologistic one. Billig acknowledges this, and he does take pains to give Lacan his due at some points in the book where it is clear that Lacan has said something fairly sensible about Freud which chimes with Billig's argument. But the very obviousness of the relevance of Lacan which arises from what some critical psychologists already know about him actually serves to obscure how much more relevant he actually is here. Notwithstanding his attempt to avoid the lures of commonsense or academic understanding, Lacan has been subject to the defence mechanism of 'intellectualisation' in which an acceptable 'understanding' of something that is repressed serves to repress it all the more efficiently. Lacan has been ill served so far by 'critical' literary theorists who have been tempted to mimic his style (and so to fall prey to exactly the kind of identification with a master that Lacan tried to disrupt) or 'critical' psychologists who only read and misread him through literary theory.

Lacan is one of the few psychoanalysts not 'to assume that ordinary, conscious thinking is unproblematic' (p. 39), to argue that 'objects of repression' are themselves 'formed in language' and that language 'demands repression' (p. 71), that 'the objects of repression' are not 'emotional impulses' (p. 184), that 'the secrets of the parents' are 'relevant to uncovering the secrets of the child's mental life' (p. 111), that 'the key lies in the moral voices that the child has been hearing' (p. 108), that 'the Oedipal situation, as described by Freud, is not culturally universal' (p. 139), that analysis should not focus on trying to 'overcome the patient's resistance' (p. 171), that 'the analyst's desires' are crucial in psychoanalysis (p. 210), that we should not search 'for the *real* memory of lost infancy' (p. 183) and that we should not look to 'the earliest moments of infancy' for the causes of trauma (p. 146). We would need a little jiggling of the wording in some of these position statements by Billig to turn them into talk of signifiers, the desire of the other and suchlike, to make them properly Lacanian. Then we would have a psychoanalytic path to exactly the issues that Billig has raised.

But then, if we were going to do that we might as well read another book about Lacan. What Billig does is to give us something more stimulating. *Freudian Repression* is an astonishing book that will probably serve to bring a psychology audience closer to psychoanalysis than they would like, and closer to Lacan than Billig would like. It is a path-breaking review of key conceptual problems in human psychology, a restatement of why an understanding of discourse is crucial to any account of subjectivity, and the elaboration of a position in the discipline against which we should argue for many years.

9

Freud and American Sociology

Manning, P. (2005) *Freud and American Sociology*. Cambridge: Polity.

A story still circulates that when Freud was travelling to the United States in 1909 to give his five introductory lectures on psychoanalysis at Clark University, he turned to his travelling companion, Jung, and declared that the Americans little knew that the arrival of psychoanalysis would be a 'plague' that would question and corrode their way of life. It is true that prospective patients of psychoanalysis, the analysands, often do not know what they are letting themselves in for; psychoanalysis subverts their attachment to their symptoms and leads them to the point where they will treat the beliefs they held about themselves as strange ideas that they relate to differently, if not abandon altogether. That disturbing and painful process can seem closer to illness than mental health; little wonder that the Viennese satirist Karl Kraus said of psychoanalysis that it was a disease of which it pretends to be the cure. One might imagine that sociology at its best would be analogous, if not homologous to this process of estrangement and re-evaluation; conservatives often dislike sociologists precisely because they unravel taken-for-granted commonsensical ideas about society.

Freud, however, was very ambivalent about the impact of psychoanalysis in relation to society; at the one moment encouraging subversive self-reflection and at the next using psychoanalytic knowledge to buttress existing social relations. If there is some truth in the image of psychoanalysis as a plague for the American way of life, it is not one that Freud would always have wanted to be remembered for. In fact, this tall tale was told by the

French psychoanalyst Lacan, who reported that Jung had told it to him (though Jung never confirmed this), and it was designed to question not only the American way of life, but what had happened to psychoanalysis when it had become implanted in the United States.

Manning's *Freud and American Sociology* is an unwitting illustration of what Lacan thought had gone wrong. It is an engagingly written book which strips psychoanalysis of all that is discomfiting, and it presents a reassuring narrative that promises that a 'pared down' version of Freud might be adapted to fit sociology so that the discipline and the individual ego will both end up strengthened, complementing each other. This can only be achieved by ensuring that sociology itself is 'pared down' to the Symbolic Interactionist tradition. The book actually operates best as an introductory text with Freud-lite as leitmotif to enable a journey through the life and contributions of Sumner, Cooley and Parsons, and via a cursory discussion of Mead, the real hero of the book, which is Goffman. Some twenty pages devoted to Goffman barely mention Freud – material has evidently been drawn from other published work in which Freud does not really figure at all – and the message is that Goffman was doing something that 'opened a door to psychoanalysis, but this was not a door he wanted to walk through himself' (p. 95).

To say that this is 'American Sociology' is thus to strictly limit what the discipline is about. Some other writers in the sociological tradition who have engaged with psychoanalysis are introduced later on; Rieff, and then, all too briefly, Hochschild, Chodorow and Prager. If Manning had shown us what this particular tradition in sociology was delimiting itself against, then we would have had a much better idea what the stakes of psychoanalysis were. What 'Europe' represented to a generation of sociologists who might want to define themselves as 'American' would be a necessary component of such an account. Instead, there are tantalising hints of what Freud outside

'American Sociology' might look like which will have to be filled in by tutors who choose to use this book in undergraduate classes.

First, we need to follow through the acknowledgement that psychoanalysis by the 1930s was 'no longer a discrete entity but a maze of possibilities' (p. 34); apart from some nods to 'relational' perspectives in psychoanalysis, there is no exposition of what the different psychoanalytic traditions have been. The proliferation of schools of psychoanalysis was once a sign of strength, and even then there are important sociological questions to be asked about the role of the training institutes in the United States in keeping some of the new ideas at bay. Unlike the British franchise of the International Psychoanalytical Association (IPA) – the organisation founded by Freud and his followers in 1910 – which divided into three distinct groups, US American psychoanalysis fragmented into separate organisations; there are different lessons for sociology from each separate tradition.

Second, we need to tell again something of the history of how psychoanalysts fleeing Nazism arrived in the United States to find that the official IPA bodies were controlled by medics who required the émigrés to undergo retraining in order that they adapt better to a form of psychoanalysis that only focused on enabling individuals to compete against each other and be content with a society oriented to mass consumption. The translation of psychoanalysis from German into English was slow and painful – as Manning points out Freud's lectures in 1909 were given in German to an audience that included sociologists who were fluent in that language – and in the process of that translation terms that appear in this book were transformed (such as 'instinct' from Freud's own term 'Trieb', which should be rendered as 'drive', operating as a force on the borders of the physiological and the psychical).

Manning comments, during his discussion of Sumner's

Folkways, that 'what follows the colon in the title of a book is a better guide to its content than what comes before it' (p. 45). This intriguing suggestion draws attention to the absence of subtitle to *Freud and American Sociology*; it is a collection of introductory essays on the classical ethnographic tradition that hovers before the door to psychoanalysis outside the United States but never shows us what the broader field of clinical practice and research has to offer.

10

Psychoanalysis Outside the Clinic

Frosh, S. (2010) *Psychoanalysis Outside the Clinic: Interventions in Psychosocial Studies*. London: Palgrave Macmillan.

Stephen Frosh has over the years almost single-handedly rescued a psychoanalytic vision of subjectivity from psychology, from inside psychology itself. He has enabled a new generation of radical psychologists to appreciate that authentic psychoanalysis is not only radically different from psychiatry, but also that we need not buy into the standard disciplinary image of a 'psychoanalytic psychology' that replicates reductive and essentialising models of individuals. He has emphasised that the arguments of a range of psychoanalytic theorists must be engaged with if we are to find a way of connecting alternative accounts of subjectivity with politics. The reference points here range from feminism and Marxism to postcolonial and queer theory. Frosh (2010) has always offered an inclusive open approach to psychoanalytic debate, even if, as he admits in his most recent book, he has a 'predilection for Lacanian obscurity' (p. 224), and perhaps such obscurity is actually a necessary counterweight to the pretence of commonsensical transparent redescription of the self offered by mainstream psychologists.

His style is at one and the same moment explanatory and musing, so psychologists and colleagues outside the discipline have an opportunity to learn and reflect on the contributions of Jacques Lacan (of course) and Melanie Klein, of 'object relations theory' in the British tradition and 'relational psychoanalysis' from the United States. The emergence of 'psychosocial studies', which provides a broader multidisciplinary forum for psychoanalytic debate that brings together psychologists, sociologists and cultural theorists, is therefore now a perfect setting for Frosh to explore what psychoanalysis has to offer 'outside' the clinic. He is concerned in this book with 'what happens when psycho-analysis is used in this way, what are its benefits for the domains in which it is applied, what are the dangers, what insights are gained, and what distortions are introduced?' (p. 5).

In some respects, psychoanalysis has long been a potent force outside the clinic, functioning as a theoretical frame for case discussion in the training institutes (which often brought together clinicians and non-clinicians), serving as a conceptual resource for social research into the state of civilization, and then very rapidly circulating as an explanatory framework in cultures in which it took root. Now psychoanalysis faces a problem which paradoxically arises from its very success. Psychoanalysis has succeeded in implanting itself in contemporary culture, to the point now that it is no longer true to refer to it as a peculiarly European or even Western mode of thought. It has taken root and flourished in US American culture, and in a manner that Lacan was already concerned with half a century ago, but it has then operated as part of the globalisation of psychology. Neoliberal incitement to modes of individual self-governance around the world now requires 'adaptation' of some kind, and the kinds of problems that Lacan (1991/2007) pointed to are still very evident, but now there is a twist. Adaptation today calls upon a flexible reflexive engagement with conditions of production which include the production of subjectivity itself, and psychoanalysis of the kind we Lacanians value is unfortunately eminently suited to such modes of responsibility and accountability.

The problem which flows from this success of psychoanalysis – the opportunities opened up for psychoanalysis to prove itself useful to neoliberal subjects searching for deeper resources to manage change and searching for ways of harnessing those resources to forge productive relationships – is that many analysands are already ahead of the game in terms of what is required of them in the clinic. This means that one of the names of the problem we need to take seriously today is 'psycho-analysis' as such. It becomes a problem if we take psychoanalysis for granted as a form of knowledge, complete knowledge or 'worldview'. Here Frosh's analysis of conceptions of the 'psychosocial subject' is apposite, arguing that even though much work in the emerging field of 'psychosocial studies' draws upon psychoanalysis, and looks to Kleinian psychoanalysis as a template for interpreting material and guide for how 'reflexivity' in research should be handled, there are some important distinctions often obscured.

Psychosocial studies aims to embed the subjectivity of the researcher in the analysis that is made of interviews, for example, by attending to what is called 'countertransference' (which in the clinic refers to the relational emotional response evoked in the analyst to particular personal distinguishing features, topics of speech or the transference of the analysand): 'What the researchers do is notice how a participant made them feel (protective, critical) without the necessary limitations of the analytic session and contract which would allow one to under-stand the validity of this response' (p. 214). More than this, the feelings and responses are actually driven by the desire of the researcher, and so, if anything, by *transference*. Now this slippage, from what is called in psychoanalytic forms of psychosocial studies 'countertransference' to what Frosh calls 'transference', begs a number of questions.

One question is why so many 'psychosocial' researchers today should believe that psychoanalysis is the touchstone for thinking about subjectivity when there are other non-psychoanalytic resources for approaching the phenomenon, with the 'turn to affect' offering some valuable alternative perspectives (e.g., Clough with Halley, 2007). Another is why these psychosocial researchers should imagine that attending to their own subjec-tivity should guide them, with studies of psychologisation in contemporary neoliberal capitalism providing some clues as to why that should be so (Gordo and De Vos, 2010). An adequate answer to these questions would surely need to mark a conceptual distinction between a 'therapeutic' mode of engagement in which there is an assumption that underlying meaning is to be divined by way of intuitive response (one of the lures of the 'relational psychoanalytic' school), and a 'psychoanalytic' approach which refused such comforting commonsensical nostrums. It is the 'therapeutic' aspect that informs much contemporary psychoanalytic discourse that flows through popular self-help psychology forums in the West (and increasingly so globalised to the rest of the world). This 'therapeutic' mutation of psychoanalysis rendered safe for mass consumption then functions as a worldview for those enthused by it and those who are compelled to evangelise about it.

Freud took pains to explain psychoanalysis to a wider audience, and we are reaping the benefits of that work and the problems it poses today. Freud (1933, pp. 181–182) did not see psychoanalysis as providing its own distinct 'Weltanschauung' or view of the world. There are important lessons here for those who treat psychoanalysis as an overall covering explanation for every aspect of human experience and then try to apply the approach to explain in psychoanalytic terms every other domain. Freud argues that rather than psychoanalysis developing as a worldview itself, the closest it will come to a worldview is when it operates within a general scientific worldview. However, even this 'worldview' is carefully defined by him in 'negative' terms, for instead of providing a positive vision of how things are or how things should be, this 'worldview', such as it is, is concerned with 'truth' and 'rejection of illusions' (ibid.).

There is another problem with the notion of 'worldview' that Freud notes here, another reason why psychoanalysis should be wary of turning itself into a worldview or even participating in a kind of worldview that pretended to provide a complete and inclusive system of knowledge. The problem is that psycho-analysis is 'incomplete', Freud (ibid.) says, and it makes no claim to provide a 'self-contained' system. We can read this note of caution as also expressing something of the nature of psychoana-lytic exploration of contradiction and division. Psychoanalysis does not aim at complete explanation, of a totalising system of knowledge, but at a relation between the subject and knowledge in which both sides of the equation are defined by their incom-pleteness.

Well, regardless whether or not he followed his own good advice here, it turns out that Freud was badly wrong, for psycho-analysis has been turned into a worldview by many of his followers. Psychoanalysis has taken form in Western culture as a series of overlapping systems of thought that are used to interpret cultural artefacts. Frosh helps us take a step back and think about the role of psychoanalysis in our work, to think about exactly what it is we are supposing of psychoanalysis so that it would appear to provide the key to unlock what is happening in economic or organisational life. Perhaps we feel a little belea-guered sometimes, it seems like we are not taken seriously and psychoanalysis is mocked for being out of date or obsessed with sex or whatever, but surely that sense of being marginal is more a function of the enclosure of our particular theoretical under-standings of fantasy located into specific competing kinds of jargon, a function of the sectarianism of psychoanalysis, rather than the marginality of psychoanalytic ideas as such. In one form or another, explicitly or implicitly, even if in versions of it we disapprove of, psychoanalysis is all around us, and precisely in the images of what fantasy is, what it might mean, why it should be contained or how it should be channelled.

Frosh encourages us to shift focus, from thinking of psycho-analysis as the 'key' which unlocks fantasy to thinking about how psychoanalysis is itself the *lock* which then has the key to open it and to confirm itself as a form of knowledge. Something of this problem has been noted by Lacanian psychoanalysts. Jacques-Alain Miller has pointed out that psychoanalytic interpretation has been turned into its reverse through the insidious accumulation of what I term 'psychotherapeutic capital', the expansion of a discourse about therapy which incorporates psychoanalysis as if it is a form of therapeutic knowledge. This psychotherapeutic capital feeds what therapists imagine the unconscious to be, which is why Lacanians now do need to 'cut' into rather than endorse this kind of interpretation (Miller, 1999).

The unconscious for us is the discourse of the Other, not some hidden material to be divined or excavated from under the surface. Lacan (1991/2007), in *Seminar XVII*, emphasises this in his argument that 'latent' content is not what is dug out from the analysand but is produced by the analyst; an 'interpretation' in psychological mode, the giving of meaning to the client, is a construction. Interpretation as Lacan described it opens the unconscious as an authentically psychoanalytic phenomenon, a phenomenon that is distinctive to the clinic; interpretation as 'cut', as 'interpretation in reverse' also opens this unconscious (Miller, 1999). It thereby cuts against a psychological redescription of the unconscious that has become a pervasive ideological motif under capitalism. In order to open the unconscious when we interpret, we need to cut against the psychologising of the unconscious. As Frosh (2010) points out at the outset, psychoanalytic knowledge is in key respects 'artificial', for 'it arises from, and refers back to, a very particular situation specially created to be different from the normal environment of everyday life' (p. 1).

Frosh's argument here is congruent with a materialist account of psychoanalysis, and with the argument developing from inside the Lacanian tradition that the analyst 'does not interpret the analysand's unconscious from the "outside"; on the contrary, the patient's unconscious is produced in the analytic relation' (Voruz, 2007: 177). The symptom itself is, as Jacques-Alain Miller points out, produced, 'constituted by its capture in the analyst's discourse, whereby, having become demand, it finds itself hooked onto the Other' (Miller, 2008: 11). Analytic speech requires address to, and response from, another that is mediated by the terms of a defined social space.

While Lacanian psychoanalysis requires a disjunction between the clinic and the outside world, psychotherapy attempts to run the two worlds together. One way of conceptualising this difference between analysis and therapy is to say that the Lacanian clinic is *in* capitalism but operates as a space *extimate* to it while the therapeutic clinic is a space of capitalism infused by its contemporary forms of subjectification. The therapeutic clinic is enmeshed not only in a moral-political context, one in which there is a duty to reflexively work upon oneself and make all others do the same, but also in a political-economic context in which the labour of the analyst and the analysand gives rise to a surplus – surplus labour which is the source of the therapist's livelihood – labour which structures the therapeutic relation as a class relation. To grasp the effects of class on psychoanalysis as a clinical practice and as a form of knowledge, however, we need to attend to what Frosh (2010) calls 'the *autonomy of the social*, the way features of the social world have causal properties and impact' (p. 67).

Our theoretical and clinical work must therefore also attend to a *disjunction* between the clinic and politics so that therapeutic reasoning does not operate in a closed ideological loop to confirm a particular model of the subject. And it will insist upon a disjunction between views of the world so that psychotherapy cannot posit itself as an all-encompassing worldview, as a metalanguage which heals the divisions between different accounts of the world and the subject. The problem lies in the way that psychotherapeutic approaches attempt to dissolve the barrier between the clinic and the outside world, and this then also has a number of consequences for clinical work, including, for example, the attempt to dissolve the power relation between analyst and analysand by the analyst disclosing something of themselves to the analysand; this is supposed to express a more authentically relational mode of being. This is not be confused with the 'relational psychoanalytic' approaches which threaten to make 'the political and social sphere subsidiary to the psychological' (Frosh, 2010, p. 177).

The very best efforts of sceptics to put a stop to the forms of psychoanalytic interpretation that circulate outside the clinic brings us to an irresolvable paradox. The more we speak about psychoanalysis in social theory and now in psychosocial research, even when we do so in ways that reflect upon its production and circulation as if it were a worldview, the more we keep those forms of interpretation in play. So, as Frosh (2010) points out, 'the issue of whether psychoanalysis "belongs" outside the clinic or not is of less significance than questions about the *effect* of this migration' (p. 5).

It is sometimes easy to forget that the psychoanalysis we use as the root metaphor, or competing systems of root metaphors, to apply to written texts outside the clinic is actually concerned with speech. More than that, psychoanalytic phenomena are a function of speech, a particular kind of representation which is itself a function of the clinic as a particular kind of social space, a particular form of organisation.

There are certain kinds of conditions that make 'fantasy' and 'affect' possible and meaningful. The 'unconscious' is not like the contents of a pot bubbling away inside each individual's head, but it appears in quite specific and peculiar conditions, conditions of speech, and that unconscious, unconscious in a psychoanalytic meaning of the term, is the site of fantasy and affect. It is not something that is dragged out from under the surface and shown to the analyst, but appears in the quite strange attempt and failure to 'free associate'. And our free association does not express unconscious contents; rather the attempt and failure to free associate, which is given a peculiar affective charge by the presence of another to whom one speaks, stumbles at certain points, runs up against certain kinds of blockage. Not all can be said, and it is what it is *not* said in speech that is what the analysis revolves around.

This is what psychoanalysis is concerned with, and this is also why psychoanalytic training is one that proceeds through a crafting of speech in transmission of technique as part of an oral tradition. There is plenty of writing in psychoanalysis, the writing is one vehicle for conceptualising psychoanalysis, but it also turns the psychoanalysis into a certain kind of discourse, scholarly perhaps, academic even, a certain kind of represen- tation that misrepresents the practice. As Dunker (2010) points out, 'there are more or less formalized structures of the course of psychoanalytic treatment and even of the clinical practice in which treatment is included. But the ethics that regulates its strategies does not guarantee the necessary passage to politics' (p. 370).

This brings us back to a crucial contribution of Frosh's work, which is to force the question as to what extent a psychoanalytic account of subjectivity is politically progressive or regressive. If it is the case that, as Frosh (2010) puts it, 'in theory and in clinical work it has rarely supplied convincing recruits to the radicali- sation of gender politics or to the ranks of sexual revolution' (p. 28) – and one must add, to the radicalisation of those working in the domains of anti-racist or socialist struggle – then we must examine very closely what is happening today when academic researchers are bewitched by psychoanalysis, by what they think is psychoanalysis. Frosh shows us that psychoanalysis is not what we think it is (it concerns a radically-divided subject, so how could it be what we think it is) and he shows us some of the perils that psychosocial studies drawing on psychoanalysis as a conceptual resource need to confront.

11

Reading French Psychoanalysis

Birksted-Breen, D., Flanders, S. and Gibeault, A. (eds.) (2010)
Reading French Psychoanalysis. London: Routledge.

The editors of this impressive volume have set themselves a quite specific task which is signalled by the title and returned to time and again in the useful general introduction to the book and in the introductions to sections on the history of psychoanalysis in France, pioneers and their legacy, the setting and process of psychoanalysis, phantasy and representation, the body and the drives, masculine and feminine sexuality and psychosis. No other book in 'The New Library of Psychoanalysis' series is devoted to psychoanalysis from a specific country, and we have not been invited to puzzle over what defines, say, Italian or Uruguayan psychoanalysis (though in both those cases there are distinctive contributions to our work). One could argue that psychoanalysis is an Enlightenment practice and, as such, universal, breaking free from national peculiarities to provide a space in which the human being is able to articulate their distress as a speaking subject of whatever language. Then the dialectic between its specific cultural roots – Jewish 'origins' and European 'context' – as particular dimensions of the enlightenment it proposes is played out on the world stage.

However, the 'Gallic Stage' of psychoanalysis has already been framed by a history of reading in the English-speaking world which is inevitably mobilised by the appearance of this book. Well-known figures from different traditions in France – André Green, Janine Chasseguet-Smirgel and Julia Kristeva – are included, and there is a careful framing of their contributions as well as convenient summaries which are marked by inset definition boxes and rounded off by a substantial well-referenced glossary. And there is another figure haunting the project which the editors have had to tackle head on, for it quickly becomes apparent that most of this work is constituted, unwillingly or not, in relation to his, Jacques Lacan. One of his early short papers, on 'the mirror stage', is included and referred to by the editors in their framing narrative in the course of the book (unfortunately in the Alan Sheridan translation), but the forty chapters repeatedly evoke his 'return to Freud' when they borrow from it and elaborate different elements from its contradictory circuitous history (this is most evident, of course, in the classic pieces by Jean Laplanche and Jean-Bertrand Pontalis) or when they set themselves against it, explicitly or implicitly.

Rivalry and misrecognition occasionally intrude, as in the misleading claim that criticism of Melanie Klein's biological approach 'led Lacan to do away with any reference to affects or the body' (p. 437), but, such potshots aside, there are some good measured assessments of conceptual differences. There is, for example, acknowledgement at one moment that the motif of 'après-coup' was retrieved by Lacan from Freud's work and then, at later points, a claim that this motif is something that would help us to define what is 'French' about these contributions. The book actually poses the question not only in terms of what beneficial and deleterious impact Lacan had on the course of French psychoanalysis but also – of more interest to Lacanians, perhaps – what in the French tradition hampered, and still mars Lacanian psychoanalysis now.

The role of psychiatry in setting the terms of debate over distress is a case in point, and this leads several contributors to pathologise analysands who do not invoke some notion of the unconscious in their speech and so must necessarily, it is assumed, be subject to pathological states such as 'operational thinking'. This kind of move is most evident in the attempts to account for 'psychosomatic' problems, which we are told in the editorial narrative is one of the characteristic aspects of French psychoanalysis. Another case in point – which accounts rather better for the hostility of feminists to French psychoanalysis than for their enthusiasm – is the appeal to underlying and universal 'femininity' (and, less so, 'masculinity') as if it were an indispensable principle of psychoanalysis. A lovely instance is the use of the notion of 'bisexualisation' not, as one might assume when first glancing at the term, to open up the way we think psychoanalytically about the constitution of sexuality so we might explore how our bodies come to signify our sex and contain our gendered experience of ourselves, but to close it down, with the promise that bisexualisation permits access to 'the male and female universes' as an alternative to 'androgynous fantasy that is toxic in nature' (p. 666). There is a deep-grained cultural assumption here about what is termed in that chapter title 'the beautiful differences' and which gives an alarming essentialising cast to thinking about 'the feminine' and 'femininity' that is antithetical to most forms of Western feminism.

Nevertheless, among the more problematic and crass contributions there are some great chapters in this book, and invidious though it might be to rank them, I would like to nominate for third place Benno Rosenberg's lucid account of erotogenic masochism and the pleasure principle which illuminates some of the other accompanying discussions of this topic. Then, second, could be Joyce McDougall's 'Plea for a measure of abnormality' (the final chapter of her already published book in English translation) which cuts against what we think we know about 'pathology', whether psychiatrically framed or otherwise. A left-field winner is Maria Torok on the illness of mourning and the fantasy of 'the exquisite corpse', perhaps precisely because (like McDougall's), it confounds our expectations of what should be 'French' about all this stuff while (unlike McDougall's or Rosenberg's) it also offers clinically-relevant material that overflows with neologisms resonant of the surrealist tradition (a tradition that also fuelled, along with French psychiatry, the early work of Lacan).

It should be noted that the frame 'French psychoanalysis' is treated, despite the 'history' and 'pioneers' narrative-ordering of the chapters, as something that should be grasped synchronically rather than diachronically. There is a very helpful diagram early on in the book of filiations which shows who was analysed by who across five generations of French analysts, though it is a shame that not all the contributors are included. The contents list gives the original publication dates of the chapters, but in the main text these are not included with the chapter titles. The reader wanting to trace a historical trajectory to the arguments could do some detective work, and the volume gives most of the clues. We have here a marvellous source-book for the history both of the Lacanian and non-Lacanian currents of work which could provide the basis for a dialogue based on clinical innovations rather than doctrinal and bureaucratic disputes.

12

The Art of Shrinking Heads

Dufour, D-R (2008) *The Art of Shrinking Heads: On the New Servitude of the Liberated in the Age of Total Capitalism.* Cambridge: Polity Press.

Dany-Robert Dufour's diagnosis of the malaise of the neoliberal subject provides a synoptic overview of historically necessary connections between Kant and Freud. The Freudian subject, who is subject to guilt, is paired with the Kantian subject who submits to ethics, and it is the task of the book to describe how that 'double-subject' has been eroded, thereby to redeem it. It becomes increasingly clear that, for Dufour, a 'sociological' analysis of the postmodern condition – Bourdieu is here viewed as an inspiration and irritation – must be augmented by an analysis of the predicament of the human subject as such. The theoretical resources are contemporary debates in Lacanian theory, and this little four-chapter book is valuable because it engages with aspects of that theory that are not readily available to an English-speaking audience. On the one hand, this opens up some new perspectives on problems that have already been explored by Žižek (who along with Jacques-Alain Miller is not referenced in the text). Deleuze comes in for criticism at many points, mainly because Deleuze celebrates the very fluidity of the subject that contemporary capitalism itself requires. There is a useful range of references to existing French debates in the book, and the book is a good contribution to these debates, and so also, as a consequence to some parallel debates in the English-speaking world.

The compass points here are provided by Paul-Laurent Assoun, and a return to the Kantian tradition in Lacanian psychoanalysis is thus a counterweight to dominant readings of Kant among English-speaking Lacanians (who too-quickly reduce the categorical imperative to a super-egoic injunction to enjoy that is to be found in the writings of the Marquis de Sade). But then, it turns out that although there are indeed some new theoretical resources, traditions of work that serve to illuminate from a different angle some well-worn debates about the degenerative ills of capitalist society, there are also some all-too familiar targets. It is here that Dufour's argument needs to be approached with care, and some of the claims teased apart. There is a string of complaints about contemporary child-rearing and educational practices, for example, and about the role of television – children watch too much of it, we are told, and it engineers a 'desymbolization' that neoliberal capitalism then feeds upon (elaborated in chapter 4). A recurring theme in the book is that liberation of the subject is only meaningful after there has been alienation, and that neoliberalism promises a fake freedom, and now a 'new servitude' that proceeds without prior subjection to another (described in chapter 3).

The corrosion of the (Kantian) 'critical distance' that enables a subject to think, to have the courage to think for themselves, thus operates through the abolition of generational differences, and also – and here Dufour warms to this theme in chapter 2 as he mires himself in some of the more reactionary motifs of psychoanalytic theory – sexual differences. So, it is necessary that adults instruct children, and that the human subject encounters a real of sexual difference that places limits on who they might become. Lacan's formulae of 'sexuation' are described as grounded in what is termed in this book 'sexion', an immutable binary that gives to each subject a genetic 'text' and a series of 'natural determinations'. Dufour thus pits himself against 'Foucauldo-Deleuzo-Lacanian' tendencies, and deviations from psychoanalysis that he detects in the writings of Jean Allouch, deviations which chime with queer theory and other neoliberal crimes against mankind that emanate from the United States. (Now we also start to see why Bourdieu should have been a target earlier in the book, for he is also, it transpires, complicit in the erosion of sexual difference.) One could surely just as well interpret the gender binary that Dufour defends as an imaginary construct, as an idealisation of sexual difference that facilitates commodification, but this interpretation would need to be developed in a critical reading of the theses outlined in the book, one in which the reader would themselves take some critical distance from it.

There is a modern categorical imperative driving the book which is that the consolidation of what Dufour terms 'total capitalism' should be resisted, but it is unclear whether this resistance is to be to capitalism as such. The name of the enemy shifts in the course of the book, and the descriptive label 'postmodernism' which is used most of the time begs more questions than it answers. What, for example, might be the significance of a third 'Marxian subject' that he mentions in passing in the first chapter as operating alongside the modern double-subject? It is symptomatic of the conceptual problems that Dufour so lucidly explores that the label 'postmodern' has already been consumed and its empty husk discarded by social theorists avid for something new, and this book has to be read against the grain of sociological work that is also structured by the commodification of its subject.

13

The Other Side of Psychoanalysis

Lacan, J. (1991/2007) *The Other Side of Psychoanalysis: The Seminar of Jacques Lacan, Book XVII* (translated with notes by R. Grigg). New York: WW Norton and Co.

Lacan's *Seminar XVII*, published at last in English translation in 2007 and in paperback edition in 2008, is well known for being about 'four discourses' (master, analyst, hysteric and university). However, the apparent accessibility and popularity of the four-discourse framework to interpret a wide variety of phenomena may have led to the seminar becoming a victim of its own success. As far as teaching and learning about Lacan is concerned, this seminar itself risks being as much of a problem as the many other problems that Lacan warns about. So, the availability of the complete seminar now alerts us to more interesting matters that Lacan addresses and unravels, what we might call 'temptations of pedagogery'. These temptations can be clustered into three different aspects of psychoanalysis as a form of idealised complete knowledge. The aspects are mastery, individuality and truth, and each aspect is organised around a series of lures.

First, knowledge is factored as an instrument and warrant for mastery, and Lacan tackles (i) the lure of psychoanalytic knowledge as something applicable, something to be employed to open the locks of both historical and personal development. Here Lacan is clear about the limits of his diagrams of the four discourses, and the dangers of using them as some kind of code through which to unlock systems of social bonds or the course of history: 'My little quadrupedal schemes... are not the Ouija boards of history. It is not necessarily the case that things always happen this way, and that things rotate in the same direction.' (p. 188). There are connections here with long-standing discussions in psychoanalysis over whether or not it constitutes a distinctive 'worldview'. To treat it as a worldview does make it ripe to be turned into academic knowledge. Then the mastery is not simply an exercise of power, but is itself a system of power within which all those who use the knowledge are embedded and subject. There is here (ii) the lure of institutional-spatial positions from which to speak and give descriptions that become intermeshed with moral judgements. Lacan takes pains to point out that the problem is not only a problem of language: '... because I am stating this from high up here on a podium there is in effect a risk of error, an element of refraction...' (p. 41). He offers a character-isation of training courses in psychoanalysis that are run like driving schools, and this brings him to (iii) the lure of complete understanding, in which there is a presumed totality and unity of a correct account. Here Lacan uses a formulation that is repeated in many other places in his writing: '... truth can only be said by halves...' (p. 36).

Opposition to what Lacan describes as a 'spherical' conception of the world becomes the basis for the connection he makes between mastery and unity. When Lacan refers to Hegel in this seminar it is often to make the point that the problem is that there is a conception in that work of total unified knowledge, as if the whole world has become one gigantic university. Here we are brought face-to-face with (iv) the lure of correct speech that ties psychoanalysis into a conceptual apparatus that will enable a form of mastery and fantasy of harmonious totality. The attempt of the speaking subject to assume a position of complete mastery, as if they have a God's-eye view of the world, is questioned here, but also questioned is the idea that there could be a 'metalan-guage' that could be purified so as to give a correct account: 'man' as 'spokesman of God' forming some kind of 'union with a woman' (p. 162). Here is one of the many links that Lacan makes between mastery, unified consciousness and masculinity. Now Lacan turns (v) to the lure of academic language and the way this language distorts psychoanalysis. Now there is a focus on the language as such, and the warning that this will afflict those who are sympathetic to Lacan and try to make him more accessible: '... the difficulty endemic to translating me into academic language will... blight anyone who, for whatever reason, tries their hand at it...' (p. 41).

The particular example Lacan gives entails a 'reversal' of his statements about the relationship between language and the unconscious. The problem is not only his old foe 'psychology' (which is thoroughly embedded in the university) but the attempt to discover things outside language, and then to insist that the unconscious must be the condition for language, as if there is something outside language that it is possible for knowledge elaborated in language to master.

Let us turn to the second aspect of psychoanalysis that Lacan tackles in the Seminar – knowledge condensed into an individual subject who then enjoys their mastery – and this brings us now to a series of further lures. For example, (vi) there is the lure of a privileged personal point of view, the fantasy of vantage point tied to agency: '... the claim to situate oneself at a point that would all of a sudden be particularly illuminated, illuminable... must not... be elevated to the point to which things were pushed by a person...' (p. 178). There is also (vii) the lure of the position of individual mastery from which to use psychoanalytic knowledge: 'The myth of the ideal I, of the I that masters, of the I whereby at least something is identical to itself, namely the speaker.' (p. 63). Lacan explicitly includes his own work as a kind of philosophy, here characterised as an anti-philosophy, in the problem. There are no guarantees that any form of knowledge could not be incorporated into certain forms of individualised mastery.

This brings us to (viii) the lure of identification with one who knows in which a student becomes tied to the idea that they too could and should be like the one who is teaching them. This, says Lacan, is also what Freud's 'myth of Oedipus' (p. 101) obscures, 'is there to conceal', for the story of Oedipus in psychoanalysis could make it seem as if there was and must be a powerful father figure who enjoyed the mother, or all the women in the primal horde before he was deposed. This then operates as a fantasy that such mastery could be attained by the subject who obediently subordinates themselves to a master and waits long enough to succeed them, to take their place. The lure (ix) of psychoanalytic knowledge as enabling the student to become more independent addresses the fantasy that it would be possible to disentangle oneself from the relationship with a teacher as master and then have access to all of the knowledge at some point: '… knowledge is the Other's *jouissance*…' (p. 15).

There is then (x) the lure of understanding psychoanalytic concepts through the intuitive resonance they have. This is relevant to some educational practices that do attempt to bring about understanding by making them personally meaningful to the student. In contrast to this, Lacan argues that: '… the subjective configuration has a perfectly mappable objectivity…' (p. 88). This 'perfectly mappable objectivity' needs to be concep-tualised in relation to his other warnings about complete knowledge. In addition, he tackles (xi) the lure of finding satis-faction in understanding psychoanalysis which brings together the points about the always already castrated father, master, and the fantasy of access to a knowledge that will give mastery to any particular individual: '… what constitutes the essence of the master's position is to be castrated… [and so]… here we find, veiled to be sure, but indicated, that what is properly called succession proceeds from castration also.' (p. 121). The fantasy of satisfaction, of jouissance that is accessible to those who have knowledge is also something that is important in current academic representations of psychoanalysis as able to get outside language and get to the real stuff beneath.

This brings us to the third aspect of idealised knowledge, truth. So, now let us examine the role of knowledge treated as a claim to be true and thus to provide a moral vantage point from which to evaluate others. Lacan shows us how (xii) the lure of finding something under the surface operates. Here he turns around the conventional understanding of the relationship between latent and manifest content: '... [for the psychoanalyst] the latent content is the interpretation that he is going to give, insofar as it is, not this knowledge that we discover in the subject, but what is added on to it to give it a sense.' (p. 113). This serves to question the idea that psychoanalysis is able to strip away the manifest content and get to the meanings under the surface. Then we are in a better position to resist (xiii) the lure that we can get beneath the language to uncover the affect beneath it. This complements the previous point, but focuses on a particular conceptual problem in psychoanalysis. Lacan notes that he is sometimes accused of neglecting affect, and points out that this is quite untrue: '... it's not affect that is repressed... It's not that the affect is suppressed, it's that it is displaced and unrecognizable.' (p. 144). This is linked to a reading of Freud, or at least to certain key passages in Freud, where it is argued that repression bears upon representation, not upon affect.

Lacan spends some time in the Seminar on (xiv) the lure of treating Oedipus as historical content excavated from the past to explain individual experience. Here Lacan runs together a number of elements of Freud's writing on cultural anthropology in order to oppose prevalent psychoanalytic readings of the Oedipus complex and events in the primal horde: '... seeing how Freud articulates this fundamental myth, it is clear that it is truly incorrect to put everything in the same basket as Oedipus.' (p. 117). This point is complemented by analysis of (xv) the lure of treating psychoanalytic forms of knowledge as historically more advanced. Here there are some interesting observations about the role of psychoanalysis as a historically situated form of knowledge: those who have an unconscious 'that had been sold to them along with the rules of colonization', those whose 'childhood was retroactively lived out in our *famil-ial* categories...' (p. 92). It is necessary to differentiate between historicism – in which subjectivity at different points in history is relativised – and the historicity of the subject borne by the past. The second perspective is classically psychoanalytic, and it also enables us to locate psychoanalytic knowledge as emerging, not as given.

Lacan then extends that critique with one focused on (xvi) the lure of treating psychoanalysis as part of the progressive unfolding of understanding. Here the political implications of psychoanalytic knowledge are addressed, first in general terms: '... there is not the slightest idea of progress, in the sense in which this term might imply a happy outcome' (p. 106). And, uncomfortably for leftists hoping to find something necessarily radical in Lacan's account, we are taken to (xv) the lure of seeing psychoanalytic knowledge as a progressive political framework to introduce students to leftist ideas. Lacan knocks these assumptions on the head: 'I am not a man of the left... everything that exists, and brotherhood first and foremost, is founded on segregation.' (p. 114). This point is rubbed home in his refusal of (xvi) the lure of seeing psychoanalytic knowledge as a progressive political framework to introduce students to revolution. Here we have the notorious comment Lacan makes about the Paris students: '... the revolutionary aspiration has only a single possible outcome... What you aspire to as revolutionaries is a master. You will get one.' (p. 207).

Finally, there is a questioning of psychoanalytic knowledge as offering something that could be sold to academic authorities who want to put on courses that contribute to such things as well-being; that is, (xvii) the lure of seeing the truth that psychoanalysis discloses or facilitates as necessarily good: 'What truth, when it emerges, has that is resolvent can from time to time be fortunate – and then disastrous in other cases. One fails to see why truth would always necessarily be beneficial.' (p. 106). These arguments are all, to some degree or another, 'negative', but perhaps it is the transformation of critique into something that is marketable and useful that is the problem we face in teaching and learning about subjectivity today. Reclaiming something of the negativity of psychoanalysis is a necessary part of a challenge to idealised forms of knowledge of whatever kind.

14

A Clinical Introduction to Lacanian Psychoanalysis

Fink, B. (1999) *A Clinical Introduction to Lacanian Psychoanalysis: Theory and Technique*. Cambridge, MA: Harvard University Press.

Lacan is usually presented to an English-speaking audience as if he merely conjured abstract theoretical concepts out of an hallucinatory reading of Freud and into an arcane system designed to mystify and seduce his readers. Sometimes this system is described as if it were an hysterical grid that could be pressed on to the tender flesh of contemporary culture, and as if it then merely repeated its own well-worn formulae regardless of the actual shape of the things it purported to explain. Bruce Fink's *Clinical Introduction*, together with his earlier *The Lacanian Subject* (Fink, 1995), gives a quite different grounding for our understanding of what Lacan was up to. Fink is currently Lacan's voice on the good earth of US America, and is translating a number of the master's seminars as well as a complete English edition of the *Écrits*. At a moment when there is a serious ambitious call from the Association Mondiale de Psychanalyse in Paris to conquer the English-speaking world, he is a key player in representing and redefining a Lacan that might appeal to this new world.

This is a great book, lucid, wide-ranging, and an invaluable guide to Lacan's work as a sustained theoretical practice. But at the selfsame moment when Lacanian psychoanalysts here might breathe sighs of relief at the appearance of an accessible clinical account they should beware that their very breath is being sucked into contours which are more US American than Lacanian. It should be said that there is an opportunity as well as a threat in the text, for odd wording that might jar on an English ear may also usefully draw attention to worrying motifs in Lacan's own work as well as Fink's. The problem is a little different from the worry Fink anticipates when he notes in the preface that his introduction might be read as an 'unjustifiably bowdlerized popularization' (p. xii). Rather, it revolves around the extent to which it really is the case that Lacan's lore is or is not 'a universal rule applicable to all contexts, all patients, all cultures, and all historical periods' (p. 224). Fink says it is not, but, aside from the fact that this squeamishness about universal truth expresses something of the postcolonial anxiety of Western liberal society and psychoanalysts trying to assuage it, the book works precisely because it is quite prescriptive and is governed by an assured confidence in the correctness of the procedures it describes. And the fact that the procedures might work does not void the fact of their cultural-historical embeddedness.

For example, in the discussion of 'Desire in Analysis' (chapter 1), a note takes up the issue of professional 'boundaries', an issue which is certainly fetishized as a universal rule by therapists in the English-speaking world, and argues that 'To appeal to a universal principle like "Therapists do not socialize with their patients" is to make a false claim and miss an opportunity to bring the analyst's desire to bear' (p. 227). An assertion of one's own practice may really be the best option here, but at the moment when the analyst brings their desire to bear they also, of course, present themselves as a robust role model who is able to be as assertive as the best man and they thus engage the patient in something uncannily close to the forms of identification much-beloved by US ego psychology.

The narrative of the book takes us from the process of 'engaging the patient in the therapeutic process' to diagnosis of the three underlying clinical structures of psychosis, neurosis and perversion and then to a reformulation of what Lacanians might expect to happen at the end of analysis. Even to present Lacan in such a linear way runs the risk that he will be understood by psychotherapists as setting out the steps that should always be taken – and already this invitation is being taken up by those who claim to provide 'Brief Lacanian Therapy' (Jerry, 1998) – rather than, at most, constructing a ladder which will provide one way up into Lacanese before being kicked away.

The 'preliminary meetings' are one of the defining characteristics of Lacanian clinical work. These first meetings focus on history and symptoms. Like other psychodynamic approaches, there is dialogue about the nature of the problem and a sense of what the person hopes to get out of the encounter. One important question, given that symptoms give some enjoyment, is 'why now?', what is it that has become too much to bear and what opens possibilities of change. There is also attention to the possibility that the person would be thrown into crisis by analysis – may suffer a 'psychotic break' – and if that were the case the therapeutic work in the preliminary meetings would continue and the emphasis would be on the construction or reinforcement of a symbolic system rather than its questioning and unravelling.

Fink does not locate Lacan in the context of French psychiatry, something that is quite important given that Lacan trained first as a psychiatrist and practised as one throughout his life. This might be because the *Clinical Introduction* is not an historical review of the development of Lacan's work, but *The Lacanian Subject* (Fink, 1995) does not provide this context either. As a result, this psychotherapeutic Lacan is able to address readers who might be wary of medical discourse and institutions even though the three clinical structures are presented as given taken-for-granted entities. Mitigating this is the openness to forms of experience that would be thoroughly pathologised by Anglo-American psychiatry.

The phenomenon of 'auditory hallucinations', for example, which is treated as a first rank symptom of schizophrenia by the DSM of the American Psychiatric Association, is discussed more sympathetically. Lacanian psychoanalysis will not distribute experiential phenomena like the hearing of voices into one of the 550 or so DSM categories, and Fink points out that Freud's neurotic patients (particularly the 'Rat Man') did hear voices. Fink is quite insistent, then, that 'Taken in its widest sense... hallucination is *not* a criterion of psychosis' (p. 83), and that 'What certain patients and nonpatients describe, for example, as a kind of running commentary that accompanies them in their daily lives... can be understood on the basis of Lacan's work on the mirror stage' (p. 85).

A little trap has been set here, however, for Fink still employs his own version of psychiatric dividing practices: 'It seems to me justifiable to distinguish psychotic hallucinations – what I'll call bona fide hallucinations – from the run-of-the-mill voices and visions that so many nonpsychotics report' (p. 83). And then, of course, the reference to the mirror stage, which did seem at one moment to normalize the hearing of voices as one of the varieties of experience in human cultures, is mobilised to drum home the warning to analysts that psychotics can pass as normal and clinical skill will be needed to detect them: 'the imaginary continues to predominate in psychosis, and the symbolic, to the extent to which it is assimilated, is "imaginarized": it is assimilated *not* as a radically different order which restructures the first, but simply by imitation of other people' (p. 89).

Moments when Fink opens up a little and displays a little doubt are quickly sutured in order to privilege an all too certain psychoanalytic storyline and the kind of culture that provided its conditions of possibility. So, in a reference to Jaynes' (1976) historical study of hearing voices, Fink comments that 'if "bicameral man" attributed them to God, he did so in the absence of any psychological understanding – just as religious people of many ilks continue to do even in our own day' (p. 248). Again, there is a balance between a cautious liberal tolerance of systems of understanding in other cultures and an insistence on the absolute necessity of a link between certain forms of child-rearing and clinical phenomena outside the frame of psychoanalytic treatment. So, on the one hand, Fink acknowledges that 'Hysteria and obsession are "structures" that, in a Western societal context, constitute a sort of great divide in subjective positions, but they are not universal, transcendental necessities. They are contingent structures based on a particular point (but quite widespread) form of society' (p. 158). On the other hand, this is then followed by a worrying string of associations to 'psychosis' which include 'a tendency toward transsexualism, repeated requests for sex change operations, and homosexual activity' (p. 98), 'the rising percentage of single-parent families today' (p. 110) and the plaint that 'more and more lesbian couples are raising children, seemingly eschewing or downplaying the importance of the father' (p. 110).

Fink does indeed worry about these implications of a Lacanian understanding of gender (and his next book promises to focus on exactly these issues) but they are implications we just have to knuckle down to and accept. After all, 'Lacan comes to see that unconscious desire is not the radical, revolutionary force he once believed it to be. Desire is subservient to the law!' (p. 207). Fink, perhaps, comes to see that Lacan is not the radical, revolutionary force he once believed him to be. Lacan is subservient to the law.

What of the analytic sessions themselves? Like other psycho-analytic approaches, the task of the patient is to free associate, to say anything that comes to mind however stupid or unpleasant. The overall course of analysis is not fixed in advance with a determinate number of sessions, and analysis may be thought of as ending when the analyst and patient stop meeting, though Fink discusses the various ways this can be conceptualised in the final chapter 'From Desire to Jouissance'. Fink presents a lucid account of the Lacanian position against the standard therapeutic wisdom that it is the patient who must want to change. On the contrary, the very nature of symptoms and our attachment to them is such that 'If there is desire in therapy that serves as its motor force, it is the analyst's, not the patient's' (p. 4). As is well known, if not notoriously so, in Lacanian practice the length of each session is not fixed, but the end of a session, with a certain average length, will be at a point where something important is said or left unsaid. The end of the session is a kind of interpretation.

A Lacanian theoretical framework enables the analyst to make sense of what is going on, rather than leading to dramatically different interventions. Books like Fink's function best when they are used as theoretical frameworks rather than as guides to action, and it is particularly important that Lacanians should not advise, interpret or guide their patients. Interpretation is designed to keep free association going and to open the unconscious to further elaboration. This means that comments which link ideas should be ambiguous rather than trying to fix things. This also means that transference (and counter-transference as part of transference) is not interpreted directly; there is no interpretation *of* the transference because this would close things down, but the notion is used by the analyst as a frame and so there is interpretation *in* the transference.

It is when we come to the process of change that we run up against an account which looks a lot more like common happiness than what we might have come to expect from Freud or Lacan. Analysis should enable the person to loosen their strong attachment to the symptom, and to find another position in relation to their symbolic world. The ethos, then, is one of questioning how we have come to be the way we are, understanding something of the key points in which we have become a subject, what our desire is, for what, and whose it is. Through this process analysis explores what relation we adopt to others. Fink's take on this in *The Lacanian Subject* is relayed through the image of the subject being brought to life by language: 'the subject as spark that flies between two signifiers in the process of subjectivization, whereby that which is other is made "one's own"' (Fink, 1995, p. 173). Lest this already seem overly voluntaristic, Fink takes the idea further in the *Clinical Introduction* where the promise of Lacanian analysis is not so much that it provides a theoretical framework to conceptualise the subject but that it may actually give birth to that subject, however unprepared the analysand may be for this: 'He may, at the extreme, come to wish he had never been born, but at least there will be a place from which he can formulate the wish! This place is the subject, the Lacanian subject' (p. 202).

The cover of *The Lacanian Subject* has a photograph of a flash of lightning crackling down to the ground, and there again is that little electric motif highlighted on the spine of *The Clinical Introduction*. This certainly brings this Lacan down to earth but now through US American culture which is structured by images of lightning as the spark which may bring life to a being, evident in the preoccupation with physical monsters made out of bits rather than individuals taking themselves apart in therapy, and a spark which will bring life to an end which is the fate of those in an electric chair in the States rather than on a couch. And there is also a powerful frontier image at work to describe where the sparky new Lacanian subject may be heading: 'The traversing of fantasy leads the subject beyond castration, beyond neurosis, into largely unexplored territory' (p. 195).

This means that Fink's introductions also read, like so many therapeutic systems and self-help manuals, as an advertisement for an individual process of taking responsibility – one-by-one but reduced to only this as a point of principle. Where there is a glimmer of social critique it is refracted through an account of alienation as always at the level of the individual's relation to others, to one or the Other. In some respects the version of Lacan delivered to an American audience here is neither Lacanian nor Freudian, for it deliberately presents what Fink (1995, p. 69) terms 'Lacanian metapsychology' as if it were a final state system.

The idea that Lacanian psychoanalysis might bear forth 'the Lacanian subject' then seems to give rise to a concern for Fink that the path we trace through the different characterisations that Lacan gives of the end of analysis may not actually have arrived at the final destination yet. Fink tries to solve this by reading backwards and then assembling the different points on Lacan's career into a coherent trajectory in which it seems as if stages in his work are mapped by 'three stages of the subject' (p. 210): '(1) the subject as constituted in relation to demand or the subject as demand, (2) the subject as desire, and (3) the subject as drive' (p. 210). The developmental narrative – of Lacan's thought and then each subject in analysis who follows him – thus serves to confirm the idea that there is a coherent Lacanian system. This rather static picture obscures the tactical subversive character of Lacan's interventions, for the contradictions between and within the various seminars and the papers in the *Écrits* are the very stuff of Lacan rather than their accidental surplus.

Fink's book provides a prescriptive and sometimes conserv-ative description of Lacanian approaches, but it is the clearest most comprehensive account so far addressed to psychothera-pists in a language they may understand and it includes detailed case studies which illustrate the playing out of different clinical structures. That clarity is itself its undoing. This is not at all to say that we should simply try to return to Lacan and romanticise an originary French source of his work, nor that we should let the English off the hook for we could match the pragmatic upbeat tone of US American Lacan with a version of our own which sits easily with empiricist discourse (Easthope, 1999). The odds are that 'clinical introductions' here will also trace their ways through forms of representation which distort and adapt him to local psychiatric or therapeutic cultural and institutional impera-tives. Perhaps it is all the better that we are able to see the cultural specificity of Fink's account. Only by striking a critical distance from any account of the subject, after all, will it be possible for us to strike a critical distance from assumptions about our own subjectivity and thus, asymptotically, to come closer to Lacan conceptually if not clinically.

15

The Subject of Addiction

Loose, R. (2002) *The Subject of Addiction: Psychoanalysis and the Administration of Enjoyment*. London and New York: Karnac Books.

Discussions of addiction too often get tangled up in the ideological preoccupations and agendas of contemporary culture, and in a domain of speculation and proscription where psychology abuts the state. On the one hand metaphors of addiction have spread well beyond the discipline to account for our abnormal attachments to cyberspace (in 'internet addiction') or to each other (in forms of 'co-dependency'). On the other hand the 'war on drugs' expands the remit of governmental intervention from the injunction to just say 'no', to military intervention in its own dependent states. The problem, as Rik Loose points out in *The Subject of Addiction*, is that attention is thereby drawn to the range of 'objects' to which we are supposed to be addicted nowadays at the expense of a serious consideration of what addiction is for the subject hooked on toxic substances; scary messages about what these substances will do to you feed the very fantasies that structure enjoyment. This path-breaking book provides a wide-ranging theoretical review and synthesis of psychoanalytic arguments that have clinical implications for our understanding and treatment of addiction.

Although Loose deploys Lacanian concepts to take psychoanalytic work in this domain forward – and the second half of the book draws on Lacan's few scattered comments on addiction and then embeds them in an accessible review and extension of Lacanian theory – his work is grounded in Freud's own attempts to grapple with the phenomenon, including his difficulties in managing it in his colleagues, patients and himself. The self-contained enjoyment of masturbation is the motif that Freud often evoked. In this respect alone, the book provides a useful historical review of the concept of addiction in Freud's work and that of 'post-Freudians' working in the area. The discussion of Freud's and Jung's dealings with their addict-analyst colleague Otto Gross, for example, is used to draw attention to questions of counter-transference (in which the analyst is sucked into the transferential relationship a patient has with objects of desire) and 'dual diagnosis' (the relationship between neurosis, which may be treatable, and addiction itself, which may not).

The advantage of the Freudian (and then Lacanian) clinical exploration of addiction is that, against the pop-psychological motifs that are prevalent in self-help books and now-dominant therapeutic ideology, the concept is stripped down and then relocated in the relationship between the subject and others. Three key Lacanian theoretical concepts are elaborated in the course of the book, 'toxicomania' (which homes in on a particular problematic use of a poisonous substance, rather than the diffuse and imprecise uses of 'addiction' to describe such things as compulsive gambling), 'jouissance' (absolute and impossible enjoyment that lures us 'beyond the pleasure principle' and against which we defend ourselves) and the Other (first instantiated in the mother but then, after the alienation and separation of the infant, a condition of desire as something human in and for the speaking subject): so, addiction is 'the incorporation of a drug which causes immediate jouissance independently of the Other' (p. 147). A fourth concept is thus necessary to describe how the addicted subject manages jouissance in its peculiar relationship with the Other (a relationship that it attempts to avoid), and Loose invents and fleshes out as his own addition to psychoanalytic vocabulary, that of 'administration'.

Apart from the historical survey and detailed excavation of psychoanalytic concepts in the first half of the book, there is a good deal of theoretical work that is of interest. The description of Lacan's account of discourse as a social bond (much of which is still unpublished in English), for example, is very clear, to the point where it also serves well as one component of the introduction to the clinical relevance of psychoanalysis generally and Lacan in particular that the book provides. However, Loose also goes beyond Lacan's 'four discourses' (of the master, university, hysteric and analyst) to formulate a discourse of addiction. This addiction discourse is produced from a torsion in the discourse of analyst (which poses a number of problems for the analyst as well as for the addict), and there is yet another twist; as Loose points out, the addiction discourse is an uncanny mirror-image of the discourse of human science Lacan alluded to (though there is a typographical error on the page where this discourse is sketched out so that the subject under the master signifier is represented as if it were a full rather than barred subject):

> In the discourse of human science, the subject is barred from his or her true cause by being spoken to in no uncertain terms of a knowledge that pretends to know without fail... [And then] addicts pursue precisely this kind of knowledge or explanation. The availability of this knowledge simply feeds their desire to know nothing about the truth of their addiction (p. 264).

There are many implications for those concerned with the place of theory in psychology, and Loose's book uses the specific issue of addiction here to raise broader questions about the relationship between pathology and knowledge (and our own forms of pathology as we relay knowledge to others).

The terrain on to which Loose takes us – from the clinical structure of the addicted subject to the discursively-structured social bonds to which we are all potentially subject – however, is the terrain of constitutive cultural representations, and an attention to this terrain poses questions for his own work. First, is not the very material he cites to illustrate the phenomenon of addiction (ranging from the testimonies of Thomas de Quincey to William Burroughs) part of the very 'stuff' (the stuffing, lining) of addiction? These representations are now historically sedimented in the symbolic order, in the field of the Other such that nowadays every subject is always already within the field of addiction. And these representations are not mere fictions through which we speak but are interwoven with material practices that today comprise the functioning of late capitalism. You do not need to be a Lacanian, for example, to argue that capitalism (in which the pharmaceutical industry is fairly important) requires crime (of which drug trafficking is quite a potent force) and that it functions, by virtue of this criminal reverse of the Law, an obscene injunction to 'enjoy' (Mandel, 1984).

Second, is not the very conceptual grounding of 'addiction' as an attempt to be independent of the Other – traced back so clearly by Loose to Freud's warnings about the perils of masturbation – symptomatic of the simultaneous injunction relayed to each subject under capitalism to be a self-contained worker able to sell their labour power but not so self-contained as to think that they can exist outside the exploitative relationships that characterise contemporary society? Masturbation is only a good emblem of the pathological administration of enjoyment independent of the Other if it is historically located as a pathology, and if the notions of 'addiction' that we might be tempted to treat as a timeless universal threat to civilization (and which Loose seems tempted to treat as such) are also historically located (Laqueur, 2003).

Toward the end of the eighteenth century in German culture there was much discussion of individual (that is, bourgeois) 'self-formation' (and it is this very enlightenment tradition out of which psychoanalysis was formed as a reflexive practice by which we might find a way to speak the truth about ourselves one-by-one), but this also conjured up the concern that there could be excessive dedication to this task. What nascent capitalism called forth also had to be contained, and it was at this time labelled as potentially pathological, as *Lesesucht* or 'reading addiction'. And now this raises a further reflexive question about the category that Rik Loose explores so well in this very enjoyable book (but not too enjoyable of course), which is that everyday practices like reading might be sustained by the very addictive phenomena that it attempts to escape.

16

Loving Psychoanalysis

Golan, R. (2006) *Loving Psychoanalysis: Looking at Culture with Freud and Lacan*. London: Karnac.

As more writing by practising psychoanalysts in the Lacanian tradition is translated into English it becomes apparent that the field of work in that tradition is very diverse, and the differences between followers of Lacan are at least as deep as the differences between psychoanalysts trained in the English-speaking world. Those differences are far deeper than disputes that divide Lacanians from their colleagues in the so-called 'British tradition', a cultural mindset that all analysts here are implicated in. Psychoanalysts in Britain, for example, often avoid all expressions of emotion – stretching the worst elements of English middle-class distance and disdain for others into caricature even outside the consulting room – and this makes work from other cultures a vital resource for reenergising analytic theory and practice. Ruth Golan's book is a case in point, and her work will serve as an antidote to the rather severe and cryptic image that Lacanians here enjoy, even more so members of the school of Lacan's son-in-law Jacques-Alain Miller, of which Golan is a member in Israel.

The book was first published in Hebrew in 2002, and it brings together clinical and cultural reflections prepared as responses to a variety of events; it could also serve as another introduction to Lacan's reading of Freud, of which there are now so many, but it provides a quite different way of working through the relationships between language, fantasy, sexual difference and the body. It would not be an easy introduction though, for it circles around Freudian concepts and images, by turns explaining and evoking aspects of the unconscious and the unconscious in culture. Golan is a published poet as well as a psychoanalyst, and this brings to her writing a lyrical quality, and perhaps it is this also that gives to the book a spiritual if not new age edge. On the one hand, then, there is a typically psychoanalytic questioning of the way we tend to seek a guarantee for who we are in God (p. 177); and, on the other hand, there is the promise of 'free choice' (p. 222), 'liberation' (p. 225) and (with a reference to Miller to anchor this claim on the final page) 'transformation'.

The suspicion of codified 'university' style knowledge that haunts the text will be familiar to psychoanalytic practitioners here, especially to those trying to prevent 'competency' frameworks from crushing ethical therapeutic work, but more strange will be the appeal to 'living knowledge that pulsates within the Real – that stems from the unknown and is exposed more and more in the course of evolution' (p. 211). Meditations on silence and testimony in the Shoah are interwoven with clinical case histories which are necessarily structured by histories of violence and memory among Jews arriving in Palestine and making it Israel. The exploration of the meanings of *Hesed Shel Emet* – 'True Grace' or 'Gracious Truth' – written on the backs of those who collect bits of bodies after suicide bombings, those who are 'keeping the Real within some kind of Symbolic framework' (p. 175), drives home what life and death includes now there. But then, as much makes itself present in this text by its silence as by its testimony. There is no explicit acknowledgement of the existence of Palestinians, and some curious references to the Jews in the concentration camps who lost the will to live who were known as the 'Muslims', curious because these references do not then connect with the bare life of Muslims and Jews facing each other inside and at the borders of Israel.

There is evidently anguish and unease at the nature of the Israeli state, but attention is turned from state violence to the 'masses' seeking to guarantee its borders, and the problem is framed as 'the language of the masses, the language of sex and violence combined with identification with the national ideal' (p. 193). And then, when an 'artistic act' that Golan describes takes place (the taking of a frame on the wall of a disused cinema in Mitzpe Ramon and making it into the pattern of an Arab headscarf), 'it became the voice of the individual' (p. 197). More disturbing still is the claim that 'the movement of radical trans-formation and liberation' that Golan hopes for will, she says, be 'characteristic of a tiny fraction of the population' (p. 222). It would seem that it is necessary to individualise culture in order to bear it, in order to take the step from barbarism to civilization. Perhaps this means that only a few enlightened individuals will escape the plight of the many beautiful souls suffering the violence which they themselves perpetuate and benefit from.

The papers gathered together here show us a new Lacan and so a new Freud and they force us to think and rethink some difficult questions. It is a shame that the translation is a little unsteady at times, with some distracting discrepancies in the spelling of some key concepts, and the separation of paragraphs by asterisks gives to the text a disjointed quality (and perhaps these typographical peculiarities actually helped me stop and think, and it will now repay rereading). This intriguing book brings psychoanalysis to life as part of culture, a particular culture with implications for all forms of difference in psychoan-alytic clinical practice.

17

Lacan on Madness

Gherovici, P. and Steinkoler, M. (eds.) (2015) *Lacan on Madness: Madness, Yes You Can't.* London and New York: Routledge.

This wide-ranging 18-chapter collection about 'madness' overturns many preconceptions about the way that psycho-analysis is usually understood to approach the topic. The contrib-utors come from different vantage points within the fractured field of Lacanian psychoanalysis, and this gives a rich diversity of accounts of the clinic, theory and cultural context (three domains of work that are signalled in the three main sections of the book as 'encountering madness', 'thinking psychosis' and 'madness and creation'). This fracturing of the field of Lacanian psycho-analysis is enabling, once the reader is able to appreciate that there is no one settled theory of 'madness' in Lacan's work, still less in the broader field of psychoanalytic practice.

Lacan's trajectory through psychoanalysis was very different from Freud's, and the starting points of the two gave rise to contrasting approaches to what is helpfully and inclusively referred to as 'madness' in this book rather than the technical (and psychiatric) term 'psychosis'. Freud invented psycho-analysis, and with it the array of concepts that turn it into very much the kind of paranoiac hermetic system that the mad are assumed to track their way around as they make sense of their own realities, concepts that include as central, of course, the 'unconscious'. An understanding and treatment of neurosis was the foundation of psychoanalytic methodology, and the existence of the unconscious posed a perpetual problem for every human being whether they were in the desperate condition of 'hysterical misery' that characterised the patients who found their way to

Freud's couch or the 'everyday unhappiness' that might, if they were lucky, await them at the end of the treatment.

The demarcation of hysteria as one form of neurosis (usually associated with women) from obsessional neurosis (as a 'dialect' of hysteria usually associated with men) made the question of gender as well as sexuality of central importance to psychoanalysis, and these questions reappear in this book. But while 'perversion' was at times seen as lying within the remit of psychoanalytic treatment (partly because every neurotic is afflicted by perverse fantasies that they find repulsive, in the case of hysterics, or bewitching, in the case of obsessional neurotics), 'psychosis' was assumed by Freud to lie outside the scope of the clinic, resistant to treatment. Later generations of psychoanalysts – most importantly those from within the Kleinian tradition – extended and transformed Freudian psychoanalysis to include psychosis within their remit.

Lacan took this extension and transformation of psychoanalysis much further, and not only because he replaced the traditional Freudian account of distress which relied too-often on a narrative of biologically-wired-in sequences of development with an account which located the human subject as a speaking being who encounters and then must navigate language. Lacan's starting point was as a psychiatrist who worked first with 'psychosis' and then reworked, or 'returned to', Freudian theory. Instead of taking neurosis as the starting point, the starting point and 'normal' condition of human subjectivity, and then attempting to make sense of how psychosis departs from it, Lacan took psychosis and the paranoiac formation of the ego as his starting point, and this quite different conception of what is 'normal' about human subjectivity gives us a new vantage point on the neuroses (and the perversions).

The third section of the book on madness and creation (on 'environs of the hole') is actually very important for the Lacanian rereading of psychoanalysis. This section of the book includes discussion of James Joyce and Virginia Woolf (by Juliet Flower MacCannell), of Samuel Beckett (by Olga Cox Cameron) and of the Baroque poet Richard Crashaw (by Stephen W. Whitworth). These readings of classic authors are complemented by an exploration of work by Primo Levi (by Paola Mieli) and of creative text by a psychiatric patient (by Manya Steinkoler). At their best these chapters shift focus, with Lacan, and in line with the trajectory of Lacan's own discovery of Freudian psychoanalysis, away from psychiatric terminology to a wider concern with the location of subjectivity in culture, with the attempt by the artist to creatively rework the images of humanity that provide models and warnings about what it is to be a human being.

These chapters drive home how important the creative process was for Lacan himself as he broke from medical psychiatry and, alongside his personal analysis and training as a psychoanalyst, encountered the surrealists, was friends with Salvador Dalí and attended a reading of *Ulysses* by James Joyce (a writer Lacan returned to at the end of his journey from madness to psychoanalysis and back again). They each show how Lacan built a version of psychoanalysis that has the potential to challenge our images of madness and normality from a basic premise that is spelt out in the second section of the book (in a chapter by Jasper Feyaerts and Stijn Vanheule which contrasts Lacan with Merleau-Ponty): 'Language enables the human being to fictionalize reality and to live it through as a problem of truth, believed in conditionally' (p. 160).

The second part of the book (on 'method in madness') also includes an examination of the importance of Lacan's first beloved patient he dubbed 'Aimée', psychotic subject of his doctoral thesis on 'self-punishment paranoia'. Marguerite Anzieu was, Jean Allouch argues, Lacan's muse and even something approaching the status of his first psychoanalyst. There are detailed considerations of 'melancholia' (by Russell Grigg), 'narcissistic neurosis' (by Hector Yankelevich) and 'manic-depressive psychosis' (by Darian Leader) that tread a delicate path through psychiatric conceptions of distress and open the way to something quite different, something more in tune with 'madness' than the reduced notion of 'psychosis'.

The existential and (most Lacanians would say) irreversible 'choice' of madness (discussed by Nestor Braunstein) and the unravelling of the category in contemporary psychoanalysis (discussed by Jean-Claude Maleval) are complemented by a clear account of the insistent connection in psychoanalysis, and in Lacanian psychoanalysis, between madness, gender and sexuality (by Claude-Nöele Pickmann). Were we to read back from the third section of the book on culture to these chapters on theory we might also be more sensitised to the way that images of women, their sexuality and their madness enter into their unconscious lives rather than simply seeming to flow from it.

There are connections between this potentially more critical (and, dare we say, historicising) location of psychoanalytic subjectivity in cultural context and some of the chapters in part one of the book (that on 'madness manifest' as the editors put it). Alongside the clinical case descriptions in the first two chapters, one about a man (by Rolf Flor) and the other a woman (by Geneviève Morel), and a cultural-clinical exploration of images of suicide bombers (by Richard Boothby), there are two chapters that illustrate how radical Lacan's own shift from psychiatry to psychoanalysis was, and how it continues to unravel psychiatric diagnoses of the 'mad' today. A chapter by Paul Verhaeghe rehearses his argument that contemporary subjectivity does not correspond to the psychoanalytic categories assumed by Freud, and the chapter by Guy Dana (on 're-inventing the institution') explicitly takes its distance from psychiatric treatment in a deployment of some ideas from Michel Foucault.

The signs are there from the beginning of the book of an encounter between psychoanalysis and other traditions of work that throw it into question, and some of the contributors are brave enough to treat this questioning as something that is in the spirit of psychoanalysis rather than a threat to it. Most often these are just signs, and there is no sustained engagement with, for example, the work of Foucault, or Franco Basaglia (a psychiatrist and then inspiration for the 'democratic psychiatry' movement) or Thomas Szasz (trained as a psychoanalyst and then critic of the medical model of 'madness'). The references to these other traditions of work are fleeting, and some of the contributors seem as certain about the truth of psychoanalysis as psychotics (seen from within the frame of Lacanian theory) are about their delusions. Together, though, these Lacanians illustrate the truth of the founding premise of the book that there is something impossible not only about 'madness' but also about psychoanalysis itself, even that that impossibility comes to define it, that it is not a case of discovering that, yes, you can use psychoanalysis to make sense of madness or, no, you cannot, but rather 'yes, you can't'.

18

The Subject of Psychosis

Vanheule, S. (2011) *The Subject of Psychosis: A Lacanian Perspective*. London: Palgrave Macmillan.

Stijn Vanheule's 2011 *The Subject of Psychosis: A Lacanian Perspective* (London: Palgrave) is an extraordinarily clear decomposition of Lacan's trajectory from surrealist concerns with representations of madness to literary attempts to signifierise it. One might even say that it is excessively clear, and that we have opened up for us in the book a view of psychosis that is as 'open to the sky' as it is for the psychotic who sees better than neurotics the unbearable nature of language and the place of the subject. At the same time it provides a viewpoint doomed to eventually loosen its ties with the 'scientific' description Lacan at times promised, and arrives at a more ambiguous and enigmatic relation between reason and unreason, to something closer to the 'babbling practice' that is psychoanalysis in Lacan's characterisation of it in *Seminar XXIV*.

Vanheule organises his account around four 'eras'. Aimée's self-punishment paranoia – the subject of Lacan's 1932 doctoral thesis in psychiatry – is located in a first era in which the confusing, distressing doubling of positions of the ego and its other is grounded in imaginary identification, alienation in which 'self-knowledge is imported, and accidentally revealed at crucial moments in life' (p. 26). The second era, and this takes up the bulk of the book, is 'the age of the signifier' in which the foreclosure of the Name-of-the-Father operating as paternal metaphor means that the subject lacks 'an internalised compass of culturally and socially viable principles' to comprehend the desire of the (m)other and relations with others (p. 61). The first era empties itself into this second most significant period of Lacan's work, and the imaginary is now structured by the symbolic; the lack of 'internalised compass' to navigate the symbolic and the forms of desire brought to life within it at times of crisis tempt retreat to the imaginary, and, better, the construction of a stabilising delusional metaphor. Delusion is a necessary space for this construction that is an attempt at cure, not a symptom of disorder. Vanheule explicates in detail the role of delusion in psychosis, of which those pertaining to the domain of the voice assume centre stage, and, in one of his almost unobtrusive interpretations of Lacan's work, suggests that the result of 'an encounter with the black hole of foreclosure is that *the Other goes mad*' (p. 114). An encounter with the prospect of paternity, for example, triggers a crisis of signification in which it is the Other of the subject that is indeed deranged, calling for a symbolic response that the subject is not in a position to provide.

In the 1960s there is a shift into what Vanheule calls the third era, one in which he needs to carefully reconstruct the scattered comments Lacan makes about psychosis to trace a logic which takes psychoanalysis to the limits of the symbolic and into the realm of jouissance, and into the realm of the real. It is here that the fate of the enunciating subject is tied to the success or failure of the extraction of the object of the jouissance of the Other from their own body. This deepening of Lacan's analysis also entails a complication of the way in which the relation between inside – in which what Vanheule (p. 46) calls the 'emptity' of the subject is a crucial motif carried forward from second era Lacan – and outside of the subject – the language they use – is understood (including the way that complication is managed by the psychotic subject); now, 'voice qua object *a* points to this immanence of the living being in speech' (p. 135). We end up with the age of the knot, a fourth era in which Vanheule underscores the way that the more 'systemic' (as he puts it) articulation of real, symbolic and imaginary in the Borromean rings – the knotting of them by the *sinthome,* in the writing of Joyce, for example – brings us to 'case-specific reflection on how R, S and I are organized' (p. 165).

At some rare moments in the book an argument on which the transition from one era to the next is threaded is itself articulated, and this argument which leads us to take seriously the progressive re-knotting of Lacanian psychoanalysis is all the more compelling for being so understated. Not only does each era enable us to disentangle our practice from medical psychiatry – and Lacan's reference to de Clérambault (cited by Vanheule early on in the book) as his 'only master in psychiatry' can be read as sarcastic mock-deference and dismissal of that tradition – but also break with what Vanheule calls 'a deficit model of psychosis' (p. 147), which eventually entails that 'the boundary between neurosis and psychosis should be thought of as fluid and not categorical' (p. 164). In place of a pathologising life-sentence which psychiatry today constructs for those diagnosed as 'schizophrenic', Vanheule invites us to treat Lacan's work as providing 'parameters of reflection on how singular cases should be approached' (p. 170).

If we are to treat the narrative of Vanheule's book as a retroactively efficient account which loops its way around the history of psychiatry and psychoanalysis (and Lacanian psychoanalysis) and encourages us to question the solidity of historical categories that only temporarily (if usefully at times) anchored its practice, then we may also make use of these 'parameters of reflection' to question how those categories operate today. The reinterpretation of all of this from within what may or may not be a fifth era which is also still Lacanian might take us to the point where we ask whether 'ordinary psychosis' might come to function as an empty signifier which facilitates a more 'fluid', less 'categorical' way of working with each singular case (in which case the grip of psychiatry on psychoanalytic practice is finally loosened altogether) or whether it extends the grip of the signifier 'psychosis' so that many more 'analysants' (as Vanheule helpfully reminds us to call them) are effectively diagnosed by analysts unwittingly reproducing a normative psychiatrised symbolic mode of apprehension and subjection. There is a risk, for example, in treating the failure of symbolic elaboration by an analysant as a sign that they must therefore be 'psychotic'; then the old trope of lack of 'psychological-mindedness' used in the British tradition of psychoanalytic psychotherapy to exclude patients from access to treatment becomes resignified such that the pathologisation of those who do not speak about their symptoms in the way we expect them to speak (so we are able to hear what they are saying as symbolically elaborated) is intensified.

When that happens we might indeed be right to say that the Other (us as Other to our analysants) has gone mad, and that there is, instead of the proliferation of forms of symbolic and variety of names-of-the-father that Vanheule describes as unfolding in the course of Lacan's work, an enforcement of one kind of symbolic that the small community of Lacanian psychoanalysts share as their own peculiar delusory system. Different 'culturally and socially viable principles' are today being elaborated in different subcultures that may serve as an 'internalised compass' for their subjects (and we should here take note of Vanheule's cautious respecification of the role of the paternal metaphor in more general non-familialist terms), and even if psychoanalysts find it difficult to comprehend how such a mechanism might suffice, they do at least need to acknowledge that there is much today that is spiralling outside the range of their own compass that guides them in a purely psychoanalytic mapping of all of the symbolic.

Different kinds of knotting, unknotting and re-knotting of the symbolic that we find in the later eras of our tradition of work bring us face to face with what Vanheule emphasises right at the beginning of his book, that we are concerned not so much with 'abstract ideas' about psychosis but with 'how to orient oneself clinically with such patients' (p. 13). This statement reframed by his argument by the end of the book allows us to see how our clinical orientation to those who are no longer viewed as always-already contained within one particular discrete psychiatric category as a kind of being takes place within quite contextually-specific domains of symbolic practice in which we inhabit particular symbolic positions constituting a space for those who come to us to speak, to speak.

19

Being Irrational

Shingu, K. (2004) *Being Irrational: Lacan, the Objet a, and the Golden Mean* (translated and edited by Michael Radich). Tokyo: Gakuju Shoin.

Freud rarely referred to Japan. There is a brief discussion, in *Totem and Taboo*, of the prohibition against touching the Mikado as an example of the 'taboo upon rulers' (Freud, 1913, pp. 44–45), and some examples of animism, magic and dramatic represen-tation of intercourse to guarantee the fertility of the earth among the 'Aino' people (ibid., p. 80); these people, the Ainu, confined to the northernmost island of Hokkaido, also figure later on in Freud's mention of totemic bear feasts (ibid., p. 139). Japan here is the exotic site of pre-religious tribal relics and pre-scientific feudal traditions, a place that will serve to exemplify the prehistory of psychoanalysis but in which one might not expect psychoanalysis as such to thrive. However, even as Freud was writing this work, papers on psychoanalysis by various Japanese authors were starting to appear; 'The psychology of forget-fulness' and 'How to detect the secrets of the mind and to discover repression', for example, were published in 1912 (Okonogi, 1995).

Despite a burgeoning interest in psychoanalysis in Japan in the 1920s, visits to Freud by Japanese students in the 1930s and the formation of different societies seeking IPA affiliation through the 1940s, there was some suspicion among Western analysts that what was being developed there could not possibly really be psychoanalysis. One US-American report in the early 1950s drew upon prevailing wisdoms about the nature of oriental peoples to conclude that 'the Japanese psycho-analysts preach one doctrine [individual freedom] and follow quite another [subordination to the collective]'; while the goal of 'occidental' psychoanalysis is the 'freeing of the individual', 'Japanese psycho-analysts (as opposed to psychiatrists) do *not* try to free the individual, but, like Western psychiatrists, endeavour to adjust him to his environment – to make him coeval with heaven and earth' (Moloney, 1953, p. 302). The proclaimed opposition to adjustment of the individual to society by a US-American IPA analyst is quite stunning here, as is the assumed opposition between psychoanalysis and psychiatry (an opposition that does still have some relevance to the fate of psychoanalysis in Japan).

Lacan's comments on psychoanalysis in Japan, particularly in his preface to the Japanese edition of the *Écrits* published in 1972, can be read as making of Japan once again a limit-case in which psychoanalysis breaks down, in which it is as if (in a dictum attributed to Lacan) psychoanalysis in Japan is 'neither possible nor necessary' (Endo, 2000). Here it seems that Lacan's interest is in the 'materialist dimension' of the Japanese language, in which the Chinese *kanji* characters (which are both ideograms and phonograms as components of the Japanese writing system) are read both phonetically (with sounds imitating the original Chinese) and semantically (with Japanese sounds layered into the character). One consequence of this double inscription is that the unconscious, if it is treated as a system of hieroglyphs, is also viewed as inscribed in consciousness; the element of signification that should be repressed at the very moment the subject starts to speak is exposed, public, present to consciousness, and if this is so then we might expect that what is the case for psychotics would also be the case for the Japanese, that psychoanalysis as such is impossible; that 'Japanese *écriture* could thus be seen as a historical product of the Lacanian "foreclosure" of primal repression' (Endo, 2002).

Lacan did, around the same time as the preface, describe Japanese as 'the perpetual translation of the events of language', and he contrasted this view of the 'empire of semblances' with Barthes' (1982) account of Japan as an 'empire of signs', arguing that for the Japanese 'there is nothing to defend against the repressed, because the repressed finds itself lodged in this reference to the letter' (Lacan, 1971, 12 May). Perhaps this proposition does then indeed provide warrant for the claim that 'their writing system does not make room for the installation of primordial identification' (Nobus, 2002, p. 35). But whether psychoanalysis in Japan is impossible and unnecessary or not is another matter. On this point Lacan, in the preface, tentatively makes a more nuanced claim that for those who inhabit the Japanese language there may not be a need for psychoanalysis save to regularise relations with the machinery of their enjoyment ('*c'est pourquoi personne qui habite cette langue, n'a besoin d'être psychanalysé, sinon pour régulariser ses relations avec les machines-à-sous*') (Lacan, 2001, p. 498). It is possible to read this statement as a reiteration of that US-American claim twenty years earlier that psychoanalysis in Japan must actually necessarily be concerned primarily with adjustment to be possible as a culturally-appropriate clinical practice. At the very least, the question of translation of psychoanalytic concepts from the West (whether from German or English, or now from French) is intimately bound up with the internal process of translation from script to script, and within the forms of script used for speaking and writing.

Rival collections of Freud's writings appeared in Japan from 1929 to 1933, and the different editions reflected not only the struggle between certain individuals vying for Freud's attention and between groups with vested interests in particular interpretations of psychoanalysis as literary or clinical domains of knowledge, but also between disciplinary traditions (Okonogi, 1995). We can see this played out most clearly in the two translations of *Beyond the Pleasure Principle* that appeared in 1930. One version was translated from the 1920 German edition – *Jenseits des*

Lustprinzips – and it rendered '*Geist*' (a noun) as *shinteki* (an adjective), for which one literal rendition might be 'of the heart-mind' (Blowers and Yang, 1997, p. 123). The other version, translated from the 1922 edition, took the supposed equivalent term 'mental' and translated it as *seishin* (or 'spirit'). Another Japanese translation ten years later rendered 'mental' as *shinri*, but this term, chosen by the leading lay-analyst and translator Ohtsuki Kenji (Blowers and Yang, 2001), has since been used to designate 'psychology' rather than psychoanalysis (Oyama et al., 2001). So, 'psychology' is nowadays referred to in Japan as *shinrigaku*, while *seishin* signifies a range of practices, from the spiritual, *seishinteki*, to the medical, as in *seishin-byōin* for 'mental hospital' and *seishin-byō-igaku* for 'psychiatry' (Brannen, 1991). Now, after the marginalisation of the lay analysts during the formation of the Japan Psychoanalytic Association in 1955, psychoanalysis tends to be treated as a sub-discipline of psychiatry (Blowers and Yang, 2001).

Psychoanalysis in Japan (with 'analysis' rendered as *bunseki*) is now stamped with this history as *seishin-bunseki*, and although the quantity of practising psychoanalysts is still quite small (with the roster of full members on the Japanese IPA group, the Japan Psychoanalytic Society, still numbering less than twenty), there is a good deal of activity and debate. There are Japanese IPA groups, which include adherents of versions of ego psychology, object relations theory and Kleinian analysis, and proponents of now well-known concepts such as *amae*, or 'dependency', that are sometimes and sometimes not treated as distinctively Japanese emotions pertaining to the relationship between the individual and society (Doi, 1973). And there are Lacanian groups, including the Lacan Society of Japan and the Groupe franco-japonais of the Champ freudien, of which Shingu Kazushige has been secretary.

Being Irrational, originally published as *Rakan no seishin-bunseki* in 1995, is the most widely-read introduction to Lacan in Japan. The English translation now makes available some windows on to the state of Lacanian psychoanalysis there for the Western reader; windows not thrown wide open so that it all becomes clear, but through which a number of different aspects of the unconscious in Japan are refracted so that we may once again catch sight of what is most strange about Lacan's work. Shingu is not concerned with peculiarities of the Japanese character nor with the peculiar things psychoanalysts in the West have said about the Japanese language, for his sights are set on the explication of 'Lacan's psychoanalysis' and insofar as there is any explicit attention to the relationship between psychoanalysis and culture it is directed to Lacan's struggle to disengage from Anglo-American assumptions about the subject and return to Freud. Nevertheless, there are also some intriguing signs of cultural difference that mark the reception of Lacanian psycho-analysis in Japan.

The first two chapters of this beautifully-written book set the scene, with an engaging account of Lacan's route through psychiatry and surrealism and then his fraught encounters with Anna Freud and Melanie Klein before excommunication from the IPA. The narrative is picked up later in the book; with chapter six tracing the formation of the EFP, chapter seven taking us back to what we may learn about the object of psychoanalysis from Irma's dream, and chapter eight focusing on the question of what authorizes an analyst (through an account of the four discourses and the pass). In these last chapters we also return to Lacan's own mortal struggle (at which point there is some musing about Freud in relation to an early injury to his mouth and the cigars which perhaps hastened his death from cancer of the palate, and about Lacan in relation to the anal quality of money for him and death from bowel cancer). The lengthy theoretical excursus in chapters three, four and five takes us from the Rome discourse to the Schema L, from the mirror stage to repetition and, through the 'fort-da' game, to the process of symbolization in which we 'become Other' to others and to ourselves.

It is through this process of becoming Other that we meet the *objet a*, and it is this object around which the book revolves; '*object a* is the support that is necessitated when I comes to see itself from a transcendental perspective' (p. 56). But there is a specific quality of the relation of the I to the *objet a* that is also the relation of the Other to the I, and this relation is something that is reiterated time and again through the course of the book: 'the *objet a* thus expresses the value of the I that thinks it is human, seen from the viewpoint of the One' (p. 128). The relation is expressed through the 'golden mean', or what Lacan fleetingly refers to as 'a basis for this little *a*', 'the irrational number known as the golden number' (Lacan, 1975/1998, p. 49). For Shingu, then, the equation that is used to calculate the golden mean is 'also the equation of the symbolization process' (p. 98), and 'the Symbolic includes within itself the golden mean, as the logical end-point of the extension *ad infinitum* of reflexive selfhood' (p. 119). It is the golden mean that provides the compass for the book, and which allows the author to place each of the elements into a rather neat relationship with each other, to the point, for example, where he can say that 'in relation to Fliess, Freud is the golden mean' (p. 149).

The European context for the development of Lacan's psycho-analysis is carefully elaborated, but there are times when the distance between the reader and what they are told about the Japanese context – the location for some other key examples – is almost erased, and there is then a temptation for us to use cultural reference points to understand what is going on that are actually a little too familiar to us, so familiar that we may be misled into imagining that we understand what is going on. In the very first pages, for example, we are introduced to one of Shingu's patients (and through this device, to Shingu himself). The patient speaks of a delusion she had that she was Red Riding Hood who has eaten 'the poison apple'; this after she listened to a music tape her doctor had given her mother to take home with her, of a Mozart string quartet. (Shingu is a psychiatrist, and the clinical examples in the book are all located in this psychiatric context.) An author's footnote to this English translation suggests that confusion between daughter and mother is expressed in the elision in her account between being Red Riding Hood and being Snow White (the character who ate the apple provided by her wicked stepmother). Even so, all of this material (and the trans-ferential relationship between the patient who is at that time studying French literature and the doctor who is then more inter-ested in Klein) is already saturated with Western imagery. And while European fairy tales and classical music could be regarded as having no deep impact on the unconscious material (or trans-ference), the architecture of this rendition of psychoanalysis is also constructed out of European material; we are reminded, for example, that the ratio of height to breadth of the Parthenon in Greece is very close to that of the golden mean (p. 55).

At other moments the distance is made very apparent, and we are jolted out of our comfortable recognition of what it is to speak in Japan. And, paradoxically, the most startling example of this comes when we are being told about the speaking subject and the Other as if that relationship were a universal feature of the human being's relation to language. The translator, Michael Radich, points out in his forward that verbs in Japanese do not conjugate for the person and that there are no articles, and this means that the use of *watashi*, or 'I', would be such that 'I am an other' and 'the "I" is an other' is expressed in exactly the same way. So, a discussion of the 'Liar's Paradox' tracks through the trajectory 'I' might take if 'some circumstances forces I to lie', at how regret at the lie may mean that 'I repents, and goes to church to confess', but then how 'If I is truly an inveterate liar, then that truth, itself, becomes untrue the moment I enunciates it' (p. 66). The necessarily clumsy and disturbing grammatical form of the exposition here (in stark contrast to the lucid flow of the text in the rest of the book) cleverly draws attention to the way that 'I hopes somehow to verify its own ideas about what goes on within it' and is thus brought to the point where it realises that this 'I' 'cannot exist' (ibid.).

But is the suspicion that the I is dependent on the Other something that is factored into different language systems – here, Japanese – in culturally-specific ways? In his account of the mirror stage and in connection with the case of Aimée, Shingu explains that a paranoiac mode of being is a necessary part of what it is to be human 'because society is predicated on the inviolability of the individual's personal integrity on the one hand and the equality of individuals on the other' (p. 103). Precisely because the site from which this book is written is so different from the world of most Western readers we are compelled to ask what kind of society is being evoked here. This issue is not so much to do with the contents of this or that symbolic system, and at odd moments we notice claims about what things mean that may not travel so well to our world – as in the comment that 'we frequently encounter the use of vegetables as a symbol for lost vitality and life' (p. 62) – but the issue concerns the conditions of possibility for intersubjectivity that are structured like a language, and distinctively so in different languages.

Take the case of Lacan's sophism concerning logical time in which Shingu sees the 'full set of structural prerequisites to paranoia'; that is, 'the deep-hidden sense of frustration and impotence; the group awareness that exists solely that we might not be left on the outer; the sense of righteousness that logically justifies the self by rationalizing one's actions' (p. 47). Lacan's (1988) threefold temporal sequence – of the instant of the glance, time for comprehending and the moment of concluding – is organised in this account around the Japanese term *sekitate*, 'race against time', configured as if it were a race against the group. A footnote added for the English translation draws attention to the importance of *rentai* ('solidarity') to 'the famous group imperative of Japanese culture, especially in the context of the modern labor movement' as the second step of the sophism, and then 'Betraying the group cause to save your own skin, or to advance your own interests (Step 3), is called *nukegake*, "to run out on" (your fellows)' (p. 47). The term *kirisute* survives from the prerogative of the samurai to literally cut down social inferiors, now to mean 'any social policy that demands some sector (usually the weak or disadvantaged) to be neglected (i.e., in Lacan's terms, relegated to the "inhuman") for the sake of the "greater common good"'(ibid.), but it is the role the concept plays in the image of a 'a team player, loyal to the group cause' (p. 47) that is surely most decisive in the required loyalty of workers to the group and to management in contemporary Japanese corporate capitalism (Ichiyo, 1987).

There are a number of allusions to Buddhism in the book, and to terms that are used in a way that are distinctive to that religion rather than being generically Japanese. Of the desire of the Other, for example, we are told that of itself, 'the desire means literally "nothing" (*kū*)' (p. 74). Some of the allusions are spelled out in the text, and sometimes in the helpful but never intrusive footnotes added by the translator. Here Radich notes that 'As opposed to other words for "empty, nothing, nothingness" which exist in Japanese, *kū* is strongly associated with the *śūnyatā* of Buddhism, particularly as it is found in Zen' (p. 74). So, for Shingu, against 'modern freedom' which consists in saying 'no' to the desire of the Other, for psychoanalysis 'freedom of desire consists in *becoming* the desire of the Other'; 'Surely, then, there is indeed freedom in psychoanalysis, if only in the Zen sense of freedom' (p. 78). This then leads him to counterpose the notion of *shizen* – something close to 'nature', but perhaps something equally as close to the Other – and science; this nature 'is not "nature" as the object of science, but the Eastern "nature" as that to which self returns, and with which it becomes one' (p. 79).

At the same time there is also another spiritual resource ready to hand at a number of points in the text that complements this appeal to Eastern nature, that of Christianity. This appears in some of the examples (one instance being that of confession after I has been forced to lie), and also in the way the relation to the Other is conceptualised. The 'ordeal of language' (p. 69), as one case in point, translates *junan* of the 'helpless suffering being' which is also the 'passion' of Christ. There is an evocative and alluring quality to this book as it slides smoothly between the realms of spirituality, psychiatry and science, and as we are shown the different ways in which the *objet a* reveals itself to be at work in these different domains we are drawn more deeply into the idea that there is perhaps a golden mean in which they will find some ratio between each other.

Perhaps there is a mathematical logic to the symbolic order and to the subject's relation to language and for the *objet a* under-pinned by the formula for the golden mean, but then, as Shingu points out, the nature of this logic, and this subject, is predicated on the existence of science; he writes that 'at a certain point in the history of science, then, the human subject thus conceived of an apparatus known as psychoanalysis in order that it might find itself, in the form of the *objet a*' (p. 140). We can go further than this, to say that if there was no history of science there would be no history of psychoanalysis, that 'psychoanalysis was not possible before the advent of the discourse of science' (Miller, 2002, p. 155). There are consequences of this view for the way we use logic and the way we understand the golden mean; if 'science assumes that there exists in the world the signifier which means nothing – and for nobody' – which is why psychoanalysis is the only practice that could truly be called atheist – then this takes us well away from the search for any intuitively-right harmonic unity of things, particularly of knowledge that 'sings indefinitely the imaginary wedding of the male and the female principles' (ibid., p. 149).

Now, although Shingu does not go so far as to see the golden mean in the relation between the sexes (and we will return to his account of this relation in a moment), he does use it to describe religious experience: 'at the moment when I perceives the *objet a* in its neighbour, I itself is seeing its I with the eyes of God' (p. 55); and he uses it with reference to our suffering and the suffering of Christ suffering with us: 'By realizing the odd fact that we are a whole, despite our bodies being comprised of various parts, we can feel the presence of Christ (again as a formula for the golden mean)' (p. 99). Another way of playing this would be to treat the golden mean as the intuitively-felt underside of the mathematical logic of modern science: 'Mathematics cuts a deep cleft between a context of thought and human action, establishing an unambiguous division of head and hand in the production process' (Sohn-Rethel, 1978, pp. 112–113), and then exact science is 'objective' because the abstracted elements of exchange relations under capitalism provide the conditions of possibility for the Kantian 'transcendental subject' (with which we may, in one of the ideologically-reflexive responses to our alienation, identify, as if in a relation to God or Christ).

There is, however, a deeper and more potent disjunction that structures our relation to this text that we need to attend to. In the final chapter, Lacan's statement that 'there's no such thing as a sexual relationship' (Lacan, 1975/1998, p. 12) is cited to lay bare 'an ontology lodged at the heart of the Oedipal subject' (p. 176), and a translator's footnote points out that the 'relation' or '*rapport*' that Lacan is referring to also evokes the 'ratio' or 'mathematical constant' that we might suppose to exist in nature (p. 176). There is, of course, a close connection between the discussions of the 'ratio' of sex and that of nature in Lacan's work; in *Seminar XVII* (Lacan, 1991/2007), for example, he anticipates the argument he will elaborate in *Encore*, with the statement that 'there is no place possible in a mythical union defined as sexual between man and woman', and shortly afterwards, in the same session, he points out apropos the 'proportional mean' that appears in such mathematical forms as the Fibonacci series that there is 'some kind of intuitive harmony', and then 'a romanticism that still continues to call it the golden number and wears itself out finding it on the surface of everything' (ibid.). If there is some powerful mathematical attraction to this ratio, then, it needs to be treated not as the site of harmonic resolution of difference but as the ideal point which will be impossible to attain. Something of this tension is well said in Shingu's comment that 'the symbolization process also holds out the sweet promise that one day the self will be expressed as one, fixed, beautiful number – the golden mean – somewhere on the far side of infinity' (p. 119).

One of the most striking things about Shingu's account is that while the 'sweet promise' of the 'golden mean' is repeatedly evoked and then characterised as something impossible to attain – as lying 'somewhere on the far side of infinity' – it is not indexed to the impossibility of the sexual relation. Although there is a claim toward the end of the book that we will look at the consequences of Lacan's reworking of Oedipus for 'relations between the genders it constructs' (p. 175), there is actually only the briefest reference to the problematic of sexuation. Throughout his account of neurotic suffering – *junan* (ordeal, suffering, passion) – there is no differentiation made between hysteria and obsessional neurosis in relation to gender, no suggestion that there may be a difference between the suffering of men and women, or of the relation of women and men to passion. That is, a quite particular relationship between men and women is elided. Even, in a footnote, when the fates of the 'male child' and 'female child' at the time of the Oedipus complex are 'handled as two independent variables', this is followed by the comment that 'we are surely required to think in terms of a more fundamental Oedipus complex held in common by both genders' (p. 171).

This poses a puzzle at the very least for how this book should be read from outside the Japanese language, for within the gaze of the West Japan is often depicted as a place where relations of gender and sexual difference are of the utmost importance (e.g., Buruma, 1995). What we are not being told about the internal texture of Japanese life cannot fail not to appear as a question about the translation of Japanese psychoanalysis into the English language, so that it is as if it is something that 'doesn't stop not being written' (Lacan, 1975/1998, p. 59). Perhaps it is not so much that Japan is the limit-case where psychoanalysis breaks down (as if it will not function there because of the nature of its society, character or language) but that it is a limit-case because the relation between the West and Japan is itself impossible. There may very well be psychoanalysis in Japan (though we cannot be more sure about that than we are sure that there is actually really psychoanalysis now in the West), but what we can make of it does not lie in the realms of imaginary understanding or symbolic mapping but is in the real. What we are faced with is a new question about the way that cultural difference is of the real. *Being Irrational* thus serves as an excellent provocative introduction to and subversion of what we think Lacan's psychoanalysis is about.

20

The Lacanian Left

Stavrakakis, Y. (2007) *The Lacanian Left*. Edinburgh: Edinburgh University Press.

This book provides a detailed theoretical assessment of the role of Lacanian theory for progressive politics. At the very least it could serve as an introduction to Lacan in political and social theory. It is beautifully written, and gives one of the most lucid overviews of the possible place of Lacan for those who are trying to change the world. Those who have taken the fateful step of trying to build bridges from Lacan to the Left will find this an invaluable text for thinking through what the options are. Those who come from the Left may hesitate, however, at some of the utopian elements of politics Stavrakakis will make them hand in before they can proceed further. I found myself torn between one side of the bridge and the other, and my complaints against this book should be read in that light, and my complaints should also be read in the context of my admiration for what Stavrakakis has accomplished here. First question: Is there such a strict homology between utopian politics – Trotsky's 'boundless horizon of beauty, joy and happiness' that Stavrakakis scorns (p. 261), for example – and the utopianism that fuels intra-psychic and primary object relations?

It is true that fantasmatic utopianism can be reactionary, and in some way regressive, but the anchoring of a political critique of this problem – and it is one we see more immediately at work in fascism and populism than in traditional left politics (in which there has often actually been a more worrying tendency to moralise about the importance of deferred gratification) – to Lacanian psychoanalysis is not so easy. There is a significant slip in Stavrakakis' account at precisely this point which betrays his own apparent wishful fantasy that Lacan says what he wants him to say. We are told, as part of the narrative about the lures and errors of ecstatic identification, that Lacan believes that the subject can be brought to something very like this moment of experiential bliss, and a quote from *Seminar IX Identification* is given as evidence: '... at this unique instant demand and desire coincide, and it is this which gives to the ego this blossoming of identificatory joy from which *jouissance* springs' (and the translation on p. 197 is from the unofficial English version of the seminar by Cormac Gallagher).

This certainly reads like Lacan, but there is even in this uncanny closeness to Lacan's own argument a crucial difference of emphasis. It would, after all, be all the more alluring an image if this description was of something attainable, something that was experienced at a moment of sexual encounter which then provided the template for what a subject might expect to be achievable in the political realm. In fact Lacan warns *against* this particular conception of identificatory joy, even to the point of contesting the terms in which it is formulated (and his refusal of this image would be articulated in later seminars in his account of the impossibility of sexual rapport). However, the quote is not from Lacan at all, but from Piera Aulagnier, one-time partner of Cornelius Castoriadis, and Lacan comments on her presentation made during his 2 May 1962 seminar that it would be a mistake to endorse her evocation of 'loving *jouissance*', for it not only holds out the promise of that moment but also implicitly endorses the conceptual separation of word and affect, a separation that Lacan explicitly sets himself against: 'No significant affect,' says Lacan after Aulagnier's intervention, 'none of those we have to deal with from anxiety to anger and all the others, can even begin to be understood except within a reference in which the relationship of x to the signifier is primary.'

This textual parapraxis matters because it signals something problematic in the texture of Stavrakakis' argument as he tries to reintroduce the domain of 'affect' into Left-Lacanian theories of discourse. Central to the theoretical trajectory of Stavrakakis' argument with his interlocutors is that we must account for what 'sticks' in politics and what bonds us to certain forms of identification: this stickiness, he tells us, 'requires the mobilisation and structuration of affect and *jouissance*' (p. 168). The appeal to psychoanalysis raises a question about what lure of 'primariness' might be at work, even in a book that provides such an impressive discussion of the intertwinement of jouissance and signification; it cues us, for example, to ask why Laclau's insistence that he has always already been talking of jouissance when he shifts the terrain of leftist practice toward discourse is not somehow satisfying enough for Stavrakakis, how it is that Stavrakakis keeps pushing for Laclau to say more about jouissance as if the 'affect' must be acknowledged as the primary stuff, delighted though he is to have led Laclau to an 'unequivocal and straightforward embrace of the Lacanian category of *jouissance*' (p. 83).

The lure of primariness, perhaps not coincidentally, reappears in the 'democratic negotiation of negativity' in 'ancient Greek democracy' (p. 269). When Stavrakakis pulls back from this to comment that 'these societies do not constitute a Golden Age' (p. 281), we surely must ask our author (who knows so well the work of negation in psychoanalysis) why he was compelled to tell us this. His acknowledgement that the priority given to the chapter on Castoriadis in the narrative of the book (bearing in mind that he emphasises in the introduction, p. 20, that the reader *'should not give way on their desire'* to read Part II of the book first, should read the book in the order in which it is presented) cannot 'solely' (he says) be put down to 'an expression of sublimated nationalism' based on their 'shared Greek origin' (p. 60). The discussion of Castoriadis serves very well as a prelude to the other theoretical chapters, and his location on the 'frontier' (p. 37) with

Lacanian theory is a compelling reason to have him here, but the best reasons in the world should not be taken on good coin if we are working psychoanalytically. This motif of Greek origins also, perhaps, helps explain his unexplicated claims that the 'European project' is 'crucial for the Left' (p. 21) and that 'we can and should envisage a strong European Union beyond traditional statist and nationalist models' (p. 221) – claims that are pretty utopian and regressive.

There is another aspect of the 'primariness' that is at work in this book which is troubling, which is the way that a theoretical framework that historically has revolved around 'affect' must be given priority, a theoretical framework that contains an incitement to think and an ambiguity about how to think it which is present in both Freud and Lacan. So, we are told that psycho-analysis 'as a discourse and practice constitutes one of the privi-leged terrains from which it is possible to reflect on this consti-tutive tension between knowledge and experience, symbolic and real' (p. 8), but we are never invited to reflect on the political-economic conditions of possibility for this discourse and practice to have assumed that privilege. The opportunity to do this occurs nearly two hundred pages later (in Part II of the book, after the theoretical forays into Castoriadis, Laclau, Žižek and Badiou) where Stavrakakis refers to 'psychoanalytic insights' considered by the advertising industry (p. 233), and even though Stavrakakis himself provides the answer to this question – 'the hegemony of the capitalist market depends on the hegemony of this particular economy of desire, on the hegemony of this particular adminis-tration of enjoyment' (p. 244) – he does not seem to notice, and certainly does not follow through, the consequences for his political argument.

It does often seem then as if it is psychoanalysis that is being put in command rather than politics, and it is the vagaries of psychoanalytic discourse that drive the elaboration of Stavrakakis' political agenda. It seems that he has followed in the tracks of the Laclau/Mouffe journey from old Leftism – the critique of crude base-superstructure conceptions of economy and ideology and correlative refusal of command-Stalinist party politics – and arrived at a definition of the political as 'encounters with the real' (p. 53) in which there is 'a lack in the discursive structure' that can 'stimulate the desire for a new articulation' (p. 59). On the one hand, then, the critique of Žižek's hopelessly idealistic (in the strict political-philosophical sense of the term) ruminations on the 'act' is impressive: he is quite right to point out that what Žižek 'hides is that his act can only assume the lack in the deeply solipsistic and apolitical form of suicide, collapsing symbolic and real death' (p. 138). On the other hand, the progressive political forces that accompanied and encouraged the Laclau/Mouffe elaboration of Eurocommunist arguments inside the disintegrating Stalinist organisations in Britain in the 1980s – feminism and pre-queer anti-identitarian social movements – are completely absent from Stavrakakis' argument.

Stavrakakis shows us very clearly what the theoretical elements from psychoanalysis might be from which we can construct a new engagement between the Left and Lacanian theory, but he seems to want to avoid all the political elements for a progressive political reappraisal of the current conjuncture through which we might know what the fault-lines are for opening from psychoanalysis to the left. And this begs a final question. Stavrakakis quite early on reassures us that, as with the Hegelian Left, there is a shift from individual to the collective, a critique of Christian modes of selfhood and an attempt to disambiguate power from democracy. It would be just as easy, though, to show that Lacan shifts attention from the collective to the individual (traversing particular fantasy one-by-one), endorses Christian modes of selfhood (in the passion of the signifier and the saintliness of the analyst) and sets itself resolutely against democratic ideals (against transparency of communication that must always betray the lure of the imaginary). Is not the requirement in Lacanian analysis that the process by which we come to terms with 'lack' an argument that another mirror version of this book might just as well have been entitled '*The Lacanian Right*'? It would seem that there is one utopian element that Stavrakakis needs for his argument to succeed, the assumption that the signifier if not the man 'Lacan' is of the left, his left.

So, if you are with Stavrakakis politically then you may quite possibly read this book as being completely in accord with what you already believe, and the book will take you further along your own political journey. In that respect, *The Lacanian Left* is perfect, complete. But if you have some political differences with him, and can use this opportunity to argue with him from the left, and even from the Lacanian left, then the book is imperfect, and then perhaps it is even better. Does not the insistence of the devout make sense here, even if they believe that all on earth must be less than perfect because it cannot stand comparison with what they believe is the Other of the Other? And for us, still, is not a flawed masterpiece the best we can hope for if there is no Other? At any measure this is a very good book, and must be engaged with for discussion around these matters to proceed.

Part III

On Social Theory and with Žižek

21

The Sublime Object of Ideology

Žižek, S. (1989) *The Sublime Object of Ideology*. London: Verso.

Slavoj Žižek's first book in English is still one of his best, and it rehearses many of the arguments that his recent work revolves around. There have been some dramatic shifts of focus over the last twenty years, most of which are a result of changes in the political and intellectual climate since the fall of the Berlin Wall, but here is a fantastic intervention from one of the leaders of the 'Slovenian school' that combines innovative readings of Marx, Lacan and Hegel and that stands the test of time. It would seem from the title as if there is one sublime object, *the* sublime object of ideology, but we discover from the book that there are least five facets of ideology today, and there are lessons from the analysis for how we should understand our attempts to conduct ideology-critique in psychology.

First, there is a refusal of our sense that there is a substantial individual subject under the surface that can be recognised and released from bondage. Instead, Žižek's return to Hegel retrieves the negative moment in dialectics, of transformations in subjectivity that are never closed over in a finished totalising 'synthesis'. That negative moment is to be discovered and catalysed in times where there is an 'act' which disturbs taken-for-granted symbolic coordinates of life under capitalism. This critique of the ideological appeal to each individual's nascent self runs counter to simple humanist psychology, and it shows how that humanist psychology itself offers a consolation for our suffering which locks us all the more tightly into what we are trying to escape.

Second, there is a refusal of the lure of freedom to enjoy that pits itself against social mechanisms that seem to constrain us. Instead, Žižek's mobilisation of Lacan's grim account of the superego uncovers the way it works not merely as an agency which forbids but also as that which operates as the obscene underside of the law, as that which incites us to pleasure, to please ourselves. This critique of the ideological motif of the welling up of libidinal energies from the nasty repression that locks them in place shows us that some forms of radical psychoanalytic liberation are as much a problem as the solution.

Third, there is a refusal of the idea that we would be happy if we embedded ourselves once again in an authentic substantial community. Instead Žižek's attention to the way we are pulled into action by a cause of desire that is always already a lost object that never actually existed, that we never actually possessed, provides an account of the fantasy that others have stolen our enjoyment, that they have this object. This critique of any authentic or balanced psychological need shows us how the retroactively constituted sense of community is organised by our attachment to an object that we will only be free of when we let it go.

Fourth, there is a refusal of the lure of underlying meaning or value hidden under the surface, and Žižek explores the homology between Freud's interpretation of dreams and Marx's analysis of commodities to show that what each prioritises is the concealment of something or the mystification of relations. This critique of contents that are there waiting to be unearthed sets itself against all forms of depth psychology and against the fiction that the correct interpretation will be the one that unlocks the true meaning.

Fifth, there is also refusal of the recent turn from a search for things underneath language to free play of narrative, of language games that trace the ideological horizons of surface reality, the limited reality of life under capitalism. Žižek's critique here is of deconstructive and postmodern academic and therapeutic trivial pursuits bewitched by the social construction of narrative. He is concerned with the way ideology is meshed into the real nature of a particular political-economic system and the way the truth about capitalism must entail a historic break with it.

These five facets of ideology are interwoven, as are the theoretical elements from Marxist politics, Lacanian psycho-analysis and Hegelian philosophy, and each facet needs to be mapped in relation to the others. This makes the book difficult at times, even though it is leavened with jokes about life under old bureaucratic 'socialism' and consumer culture and is often also very enjoyable. So, here in this ground-breaking study we have an amazing critique at one and the same time of the illusion that there is, under the surface or even in the play of narrative on the surface, a meaningful self yearning to enjoy freedom in community with others; and one point that emerges from Žižek's repetitive circling around these themes is that one of the most potent sublime objects of ideology now is psychology itself.

22

The Parallax View

Žižek, S. (2006) *The Parallax View*. Cambridge, MA: MIT Press.

The digested read digested first: The long-promised 'magnum opus' by Žižek is a delightful rich chocolaty confection at first bite but melts by the end into another warm soup of already circulating offcuts, this time in which Bartleby comes into view not waving but drowning.

The first thing we should notice about Bartleby, the protagonist of Melville's grim tale of the man who said 'I would prefer not to' in response to organisational demands, is that his refusal led to him being carted away by the police and dying as a vagrant refusing life itself. Perhaps he provides a fitting heroic figure for Deleuze, to whom we owe his second life in the world of social theory, but it beggars belief as to why this deliberately individualistic strategy of non-resistance should be taken up and championed by Žižek in his latest book. The famous psychoanalytic 'act' that Žižek has often used as a template for revolutionary disturbance of the symbolic coordinates of a situation has never been sufficiently theorised by him as applicable to collective action, and so perhaps it does make sense for him now to see Bartleby as just the latest in a series of figures – Antigone, Medea, Sethe – who stubbornly hold to their own desire (and not at all, note, the desire of the Other) and pay the price. Even if Bartleby is not a woman, in contrast to the other heroic hysterics Žižek seems to idealise, at least he is suitably feminised by the end of the tale: abject miserable victim of the legal chambers whose very reason for his resistance remains as much a mystery to the reader as to his colleagues.

The paradox is that Žižek does actually bring alive and

reenergise theoretical resources for thinking about compliance and resistance at the level of the individual and the social and, crucially, at the intersection of the two. His meditations on dialectics and negation always emphasise that we must move beyond the horizon of contemporary ideological fascination with bourgeois democracy that grips academics as well as ex-leftists in the field of politics. He opens up as much as he closes down, and that is a good deal more than much complacent 'critical' theory does. The paradox is articulated by Žižek in this book through one of his favourite examples from Lévi-Strauss: the Winnebago tribe consist of two subgroups that describe the ground-plan of the village in quite different ways. In a striking lesson for those working on the spatial distribution of management structures, we find that while one group perceives the village as consisting of an inner circle surrounded by a naturally-occurring second circle, the other group views the village as being split down the middle. For Žižek, this is no mere anthropological fairy tale which is a curiosity of life in the Great Lakes, but spells out the universal 'fundamental antagonism' of human relationships that in capitalist society must be spelt out as 'class struggle'.

The fundamental antagonism elaborated in this book, and signalled in the title, is 'parallax', and this is the conceptual core of Žižek's argument. Against any wholesome knowledge that would pretend to give an overall inclusive account of the functioning of social systems, or any policy of 'social inclusion' that would honour the sum of identities of the various communities that comprise a polity, Žižek shows us how and why an individual and the social is riven by contradiction. The contradictory antagonistic nature of reality is such that every commonsensical or theoretical view is structured by the position from which we speak about it. An employer's imperative to increase productivity and ensure the cohesion of the interrelationships between workers and management is incompatible with the historical materialist view that the 'common goal' to which the company is committed must be fractured if workers' self-management is to slough off the parasitic ruling layers who profit from the labour of others.

The implication of the parallax view – a political vision of the limits of liberal consensus on which Žižek has elaborated many times before – is not only that there is a mutually unintelligible clash of perspectives between exploiters and exploited, but that one of the stakes of the disagreement between them is that disagreement between them is necessary and inevitable. Those who rule must believe that it is possible to resolve the differences of perspective or value them equally as a meaningful cluster of opinions to be generously acknowledged and tolerated. Those who are ruled – and this is where Žižek is surely right and where his contribution to organisation studies is so valuable – must insist that there is no common measure between different perspectives and that it is possible to show why the necessary false consciousness that inhabits the worldview of the ruling class must be dispelled.

In the course of the book, as Žižek guides us through domains of philosophy and social theory holding to the red thread of 'parallax' to undermine all claims to unity of perspective, we are still left with one key parallax that haunts his own writing. The term 'parallax', which Žižek borrows from Kōjin Karatani (a revolutionary Japanese theorist of the specific necessary antinomy between the economic and the political in Kant and Marx), is deployed time and again to account for disparities between different theoretical accounts. The spatial, temporal and erotic modes of parallax (outlined on page 10) are intriguing and productive ways of extrapolating from Karatani's original conception, but we are very quickly drawn into exorbitant claims that the 'act' operates in a 'parallax gap' between the aesthetic and the religious and then that Christ occupies the parallax gap between God and man (on page 105).

The notion of parallax enables Žižek to rework his account of anamorphosis drawn from Lacan's *Seminar XI*, which was then used to show why it is only possible to 'look awry' at *objet petit a* and, by implication, at social phenomena. Parallax is now both an opening to some theoretical innovations and, at the same time, a cover for theoretical inconsistencies, contradictions in Žižek's work, particularly around the extrapolation of (a version of) Lacanian clinical practice to politics. The question is whether these contradictions can be conceptualised dialectically (as he sometimes promises) or whether the term 'parallax' will simply be used by Žižek and his followers to suture the gaps between academic, clinical and political spheres of elaboration.

The key parallax to be noted here is that Žižek is an individual theorist who privileges the romantic refusal of institutions and who idealises the 'act' of those who are willing to lose everything. And then, collectivity itself, from that perspective, is rendered into something suspect which always threatens to subordinate heroic thought to a single worldview. It may be that Žižek will eventually take a step beyond the position on one side of the divide – a position that is conceptually paralysing his work and which is resulting in repetitive complaint in recent books – but we must hope that when he does so, it is not on the model of Bartleby. For that way disaster will follow, for him and for us.

23

Žižek, Theology, Psychoanalysis and Trauma

Kotsko, A. (2008) *Žižek and Theology*. London: Continuum.

Pound, M. (2007) *Theology, Psychoanalysis and Trauma*. London: SCM Press.

Pound, M. (2008) *Žižek: A (Very) Critical Introduction*. Grand Rapids, MI: Eerdmans Publishing Co.

Religious motifs are more obviously at work in the history of philosophy than in psychoanalysis, but there are now claims that Lacan 'Christianised' Freud, and Slavoj Žižek for one drives home the idea that in Lacanian psychoanalysis we might wipe the slate clean for a new beginning in the cure and that this process gives rise to a new 'universality'. 'Introductions' to Žižek abound, and those true to the spirit of his writing repay the pleasure of reading his work with an appropriately idiosyncratic and passionate argument about how we should make sense of the contradictions and shifts of direction between books, between chapters and even sometimes between the lines. Adam Kotsko's *Žižek and Theology* traces a new line through Žižek, and shows us why we need to know something about theology in order to understand his work and why theologians should take Žižek seriously. Kotsko's aim is to clarify Žižek's claim that 'to become a true dialectical materialist, one should go through the Christian experience' (Kotsko, 2008, p. 2), and he does successfully explain why we need this book, another introduction that attends to this claim.

Kotsko provides an excellent review of Žižek's writing on

ideology and subjectivity before turning to the core of the book, two intriguing chapters on 'The Christian Experience' and on dialectical materialism. As he acknowledges, Žižek does give a classically Hegelian 'supersessionist' account of the relationship between Judaism and Christianity, but to claim that over the course of his three books on Christianity his 'esteem for Judaism steadily grows' (ibid., p. 88) is to miss the way philo-Semitism often functions as the flipside of anti-Semitism. Margaret Thatcher's comment to Jewish community leaders in her constituency that 'there are two great religions in the world, yours and mine' also neatly captures how a Christian concordat with the chosen people tends to shut out those from other religions. Kotsko approvingly notes that Žižek has said nicer things about Buddhism recently (though he has still been fairly robust about the reactionary role of His Holiness the Dalai Lama), but there is silence in the book about Žižek's oft-repeated sideswipes at Islam as being 'particularist'. (Actually, we can find, within *In Defence of Lost Causes* for example, some quite interesting and more appreciative reflections on Islam.)

The last stretch of the book, on theological responses to Žižek, takes us, most of us I suspect, into some unfamiliar territory where we learn, for example, of Roman Catholic disapproval of his critique of church institutions and Anabaptist delight at his enthusiasm for radical renunciation. There are, throughout the book, references to concepts from theological texts that conjure up other worlds of debate about the nature of modern subjectivity, with signifiers like 'the cross' that are clearly more replete with signification than we might at first glance guess. Kotsko helps non-Christians appreciate how far Žižek is immersed in these other worlds, and the complexity and depth of his argument for a dialectical materialist standpoint.

Lenin once remarked of the debate between Christians and Marxists that this was a debate with progressive effects for the former but reactionary consequences for the latter. This insightful and lucid book introduces us to another way of reading and repeating Lenin's argument; subjectivity can be theoretically invested with a concern with spirituality precisely so it can then be more effectively emptied of the Christian experience itself. We 'go through' the experience vicariously in this book, and perhaps it would be possible to view our trajectory through the text as a traversal of the fantasy of redemption for all that Christianity promises. This is a journey that Žižek himself seems to be taking, and so this book provides much more than an 'introduction', as well anticipating where our hero may be going next.

Marcus Pound, in contrast, is determined to steer Žižek back to Christianity and his *Žižek: A (Very) Critical Introduction* champions a fundamentalist Catholic reading – from out of the 'radical orthodoxy' school Kotsko helpfully describes – of Lacan against Žižek's 'crudely Protestant' (to borrow a phrase from Pound) bid to seize theological ground from the enemy, that is, from those who really do believe in God. Pound's problem with Žižek, of course, is that the sequence 'Lacan, Hegel, Marx' is eventually punctuated by the last figure in the series, and so resolves itself into atheism. For Žižek, detailed readings of Biblical texts are part of a game in which the reader is lured into something they did not expect, away from any religion whatsoever. Pound wants none of this, and he is playing a quite different game that includes pitting an ostensibly Catholic Lacan against Žižek.

Here Pound is extending an earlier reading of Lacan in his engaging and passionately argued *Theology, Psychoanalysis and Trauma*, published by SCM (the Student Christian Movement publishing outfit), in which he argues that Lacan's 'postmodern' variation on psychoanalysis 'provides the most coherent language' to 'communicate the mystery of transubstantiation within our cultural milieu' (Pound, 2007, p. xiii). We need, he insists, to appreciate how 'the liturgy of the Eucharist is analogous to analysis', because it facilitates 'subjective reflection upon the truth' (ibid., p. 155). Lacan is read through Kierkegaard, and this Christian thinker still shadows the account given in the Žižek book. St Thomas Aquinas is also present in both books. Lacan's insistence that his children be baptised and the dedication of his 1932 doctoral thesis to his Benedictine priest brother as his 'brother in religion' are summoned as evidence that Lacan's version of psychoanalysis Christianises Freud's work. There is the rather surprising claim that 'Freud already conceived of psychoanalysis as a secular form of theology' (ibid., p. 1), and once we have accepted this we are on the preferred terrain of radical orthodoxy's interventions into philosophy, one in which theological suppositions structure the relationship between the two disciplinary domains.

In the Žižek book Pound, true to form, inscribes the 'return to Freud' in the Jesuit traditionalist and universalist 'return to sources' in France from the 1930s to the 1950s: 'Lacan's return to Freud was an instance of this theological *ressourcement*' (Pound, 2008, p. 75). This is faithful to the radical orthodoxy line, that a return to medieval roots of Christianity will circumvent the Franciscan John Duns Scotus' false separation of the worlds of theology and science. We are then also back to the supersessionist motif that Catholic theologians wriggle around but eventually endorse, which is that there is a key progressive historical shift from Judaism to Christianity; one marked by Thomas Aquinas as the shift from a religious worldview in which the truth of God is as yet deficient – that is, Jewish 'old law' – to one in which it is superabundant, in which the sacrament must function as a kind of filter for those subject to 'new law' who would otherwise be blinded by the truth: 'Aquinas situates religion on the side of the symbolic and God on the side of the real' (ibid., p. 63).

Catholic 'feminist' writing – which, as Pound acknowledges, has, in some variants, included warrant for anti-Semitism – is tactically mobilised in a reading of Lacan's formulae of sexuation in order to set up an opposition between 'the Jewish God [which] conforms to the structure of masculinity' and Christianity as 'the religion of love' (ibid., p. 114). (Both Pound and Kotsko describe Lacan's formulae as marking an opposition between 'feminine' and 'masculine' gender positions, and this risks obscuring the quite deliberate reference to sexual difference in *Seminar XX*.)

Despite the attempt to outflank Žižek with a Lacan more Lacanian than Lacan himself, Pound wants to have his Eucharist and eat it, and this requires a reading of Lacan that replaces the negative moment in psychoanalysis – castration, cut off the signifier, retroactive constitution of a supposed original access to jouissance – with a real fullness of being from which we have fallen. Pound inveighs against 'Nothing' as a warrant for nihilism; a master signifier in his writing, and that of his radical orthodoxy mentors Conor Cunningham and John Milbank (with whom Žižek has recently debated in a recent book on Christianity), is 'ontology', sometimes 'onto-theology'. This might account for why he characterises Lacan's 'subject of the enunciation' as corresponding to the real as if it were something of substance.

Pound's well-written wilful misreading of Lacan allows him to argue for the human subject as 'already graced and participatory in God' rather than, as in Žižek and Lacan, being led to a 'rupture of grace' in a broken world (ibid., pp. 82–83), a rupture in a political act (for Žižek), or at the end of analysis (for Lacan). Žižek's afterword provides a succinct outline of the importance of negativity, and neatly evokes and then subverts the appeal to the 'New' testament over the 'Old' with a characteristic reading of *Psycho* in which the 'New' would be the world of Norman Bates the killer in thrall to the dead mother. Pound's Žižek book is worth reading for this afterword alone. This is dire stuff, and perhaps the best way through it is to start with Kotsko's introduction and then skip straight to Žižek's piece to clear the mind, to traverse in the most painless way these regressive fundamentalist fantasies.

24

Žižek's Politics

Dean, J. (2006) *Žižek's Politics*. London and New York: Routledge.

Jodi Dean's *Žižek's Politics* is the first book-length attempt to systematize Žižek's work. In some respects it is a success, presenting a clear rationale for the use of the category of 'enjoyment' and tracing through how Žižek employs this notion to analyse different social formations. Here Dean has a good grasp of key concepts, and the book could function as a useful guide to readers who have already bought into Žižek's cultural analysis and want to know how the different concepts could be articulated. She rehearses descriptions of the 'theft of enjoyment' and the function of 'transgression' very well, and it really seems at times as if all the different aspects of Žižek's meditations on enjoyment can be woven into one seamless web. Even so, her avoidance of certain topics as well the selection of others makes a defence of what she claims to be the 'underlying system' (p. xx) of Žižek's work much easier, too easy. The gaps are plugged by what appears to have been the late inclusion of references to Žižek's latest book on 'parallax', and this must have been a blessing, for she is then able, with him, to account for 'perspectival shifts in his own work' (p. 53).

The book is as good as Žižek at his best when the 'system' is being cobbled together, and often much more plausible than Žižek himself because Dean follows a single-track train of analysis and hooks together the different elements into a theoretical narrative. However, the book comes off the rails when she tries to show how the theoretical 'system' plays out in the realm of political action. It is then that we start to see that she has made a big mistake; the first step was to overgenerously detect some underlying ground-plan in Žižek's politics, and this then leads to some desperate stumbling over Žižek's adventures in the real world.

There are clues that it is going to end badly from early on when she follows Žižek faithfully in a complaint that the 'new social movements associated with feminism, gay activism and anti-racism' have failed to bring about 'a new world of freely self-creating identities' (p. 2). That settles that, unless you ask activists whether they do actually think that they have succeeded – those who still adhere to boring old revolutionary socialist politics will say no – and whether that kind of new world was ever on the agenda before the liberal leadership of those 'movements' were bought off. Dean seems happy to parrot her mentor instead of thinking through the political stakes of the argument right from the start with the aid of some genuinely radical political history. She then even goes so far as to cite 'feminist struggles over the right to an abortion' (p. 116) as an instance of 'depoliticization' (which, she says, go along with demands for marriage benefits for same-sex couples and media campaigns in favour of networks targeting black audiences) – a rather clueless, if not dangerous, stance to take in a country where the far-right do mobilise to bomb clinics that allow women the right to choose instead of the church or the state.

The fateful phrase 'challenge of freedom' appears in chapter one (p. 21), and it is not long after that the 'Bartleby politics' Žižek vaunts in his recent account of the 'parallax view' is described as a way of turning 'an impossibility into the possibility that things might be otherwise' (p. 29). The problem here is twofold; first, merely saying 'I would prefer not to' is likely to land an individual in an institution and an early death (as it does Bartleby himself) with erstwhile comrades left behind who are mystified by what is going on – read the Melville story, and you will find that it amounts to grim and futile (anti-)'politics'; second, it is actually quite inconsistent with what Dean seems to be adopting as the main message from Žižek's work, which is that we should accept the 'challenge of freedom' by dissolving ourselves into the law. It is 'only when we submit to the rule of law' (p. 163), she says, that we will meet this challenge, and this requires 'full surrender to the law, with no exception' (p. 165). And, god help us, here she follows Žižek's 'idea that Pauline love fulfils the law as it renders the law non-all' (p. 168). The 'no exception' and 'non-all' are cryptic Lacanian code-words here, but since Dean does not spell out their secret meaning we are at the mercy of Žižek's gloss on the theoretical notions he has absorbed on his long march.

In a book that is supposed to be about politics, Dean is very shy about being specific, and does not tell us, for example, whether this would include laws prohibiting abortion (which women are, she implies, wrong to put their energies into contesting). Why not, then, 'refuse to accept imaginary and symbolic reassurance and undergo subjective destitution' (p. 44)? If the implication is not actually that we should do this each day before breakfast, Dean does at least make it seem as if this, first, can be done outside analysis and that, second, this analytic process will serve us in the place of politics. Despite the claim that Žižek is helpful in providing 'political theorists' with 'concepts' (p. 45), we have to wait a long time for any practical political proposals; and when these are hinted at it is clear that we are going to be in deep trouble if we take them seriously. This is a desperately loyal book, and so the moments when Dean draws back and fails the test – the 'challenge of freedom' that would mean following Žižek all the way – are all the more striking. Those moments when she has to own up to her queasiness at going along with some of his analyses reveal something of the good political sense that perhaps lies submerged in this consistent 'systematic' narrative produced by a writer who is evidently transfixed by her subject. There are some minor scruples and attempts to tidy things up. She argues for the concept of 'displaced mediator' in place of 'vanishing mediator' to account for the role that Protestantism played in the triumph of capitalism (p. 111), and this because there is patently still a virulent Protestant fundamentalist tradition in the United States – a fair point which finesses Žižek's use of Jameson's theoretical notion. There are some worries about some of Žižek's contradictory political assessments of Stalinism. She says he 'neglects biopolitical aspects of Stalinism' (p. 85) – a pretty feeble criticism after she has just a few pages earlier lauded his claim that 'the brutal violence of Stalinism testifies to the authenticity of the Russian Revolution' (p. 81). She says that he is 'not always consistent' in the terms he uses to analyse fascism and Stalinism, but once again puts this down to the 'parallax gap' (p. 52), the handy most-recent get-out-of-jail card our hero has up his sleeve – and so this sutures over that little problem. There are more serious worries that bring her close to the wicked multiculturalist liberal feminism Žižek inveighs against. She does not like Žižek's reference to sadomasochistic lesbian couples as evidence that 'contemporary subjectivities' are confronting an obscene need for domination and submission – this is, she says, 'an instance of where Žižek's own enjoyment irrupts into the text' (p. 43). She has qualms about the string of examples Žižek gives of an 'act', saying that his examples 'have their drawbacks' because they are 'actually the sacrifice of someone else', and she does notice that in his examples 'the bodies are feminine and infantile' (p. 169) – but she does not follow through the political implications of this criticism. She does not like 'Bartleby politics' when it would prefer not to send aid to 'Black orphans in Africa', 'to prevent oil-drilling in a wildlife swamp', or to 'send books to educate our liberal-feminist-spirited women in Afghanistan' (these quotes with which she disagrees are from Žižek), but she then comes up with the most liberal reason not to agree with him: that we might be able to prevent a catastrophe 'for those who might be left alone and unsupported' (p. 131); this, rather than bringing to bear some political analysis of how feminism – in the activity of the Revolutionary Association of the Women of Afghanistan, for example – has operated as a form of genuine political resistance to both the Taliban and to the US-led occupation.

At some points she is forced to confront some serious obstacles to her belief in her guide. She does notice that the political-economic system is 'rife with multiple deadlocks' (p. 193) rather than fracture and an 'act' appearing at one symptomatic point, and this leads her to the more serious general point, that 'Žižek's claim regarding the depoliticized economy as the disavowed fundamental fantasy does not follow from his account of the arrangement of enjoyment in contemporary ideological formations' (p. 193). At issue here is the relationship between politics and the economy, and worries about whether Žižek is 'insufficiently materialist' (p. 188) are the least of the problem – but once again, although his 'two lines of argumentation do not link up', the inconsistency can be explained through reference to the 'parallax gap' (p. 194). This sum total of instances where Dean demurs with Žižek are cited here to indicate the degree to which she holds fast to her argument that it all must fit together, that he must make sense.

The closest we come to actual political proposals is that we should combine Žižek's idea of the 'act' – 'the violent disturbance or breaking through of the given order' – with the 'revolutionary-political Party' which will retroactively give form to the act; 'there cannot,' she argues, 'be one without the other' (p. 180). It would seem, from the way concepts are accumulated in Dean's narrative, that some of the key notions have arrived late and are designed to plug the gaps – parallax gaps no doubt – in Žižek's work. There are many points in the early chapters, for example, where we might ask why the wonderful theoretical device of 'the Party' was not brought in to solve some problems of political analysis. So, when Žižek is cited as 'prioritizing' class struggle (p. 59), we might wonder if 'the Party' might be of some use there. It seems it is not, and that for Dean 'the Party' is, instead, an entirely abstract notion that is not intended to be anchored in any actual political terrain.

Making good her claim to be light with the Lacanian theory in this book – a convenient ploy to make the 'underlying system' freer of contradiction – she very quickly asserts that class struggle for Žižek is what 'sexual difference' is for Lacan (p. 60), and so from now on we most probably will be treated to secondary-source Žižekians not only not bothering to read Lacan, but instead utilising this book for transliterating psychoanalytic theory directly into politics. Well, effectively away from politics altogether. When she says that 'it is necessary to undertake the slow, difficult work of building something new' (p. 87), 'the Party' does not then seem to occur to her either – and that might be because she sees this 'Party' – even, it seems, 'the Leninist Party' (p. 91) – as something which only formalises an 'act' after it has happened and so is not really worth bothering with before anything dramatic has taken place. If we connect Dean's enthusiastic embrace of the law with her belief in 'the Party', we arrive at the rather strange formulation that then 'identification is with the Real Other' (p. 201). Is this identification with enjoyment? After bad ideological enjoyment that this identification replaces? Before full flowering of good enjoyment in paradise? This is starting to turn into a pretty mess by the end of the book.

What Dean refused to recognise, and this might be because she treats Žižek as the new best complete theoretical package to be washed up on the shores of thoroughly depoliticised English-speaking academic 'theory', is that Žižek's writing is a bricolage of vantage points gathered together from different writers. Dean is absolutely right when she says that 'Žižek is trying to clear out a space for radical politics' (p. 49), and he is indeed battling valiantly against the liberal bourgeois democratic hegemonic forces in contemporary intellectual debate. It is necessary to affirm what is radical in Žižek's interventions against this kind of vision of his work, and to do that involves some critical assessment. When he turns the different scattered vantage points he discusses towards politics he does so as a master tactician, and this mastery includes the ability to cover his tracks and play with the naivety of his audience in the universities.

Does Dean really believe that Žižek will show her how to find ways 'to attach ourselves to law through belief in the founding dream' (p. 177), and that this then 'opens up the possibility of an enjoyment or love beyond the law' (p. 172)? There will undoubtedly be others who will be just as bedazzled by such promises, and many more bewitched by the motif of 'parallax' as a theoretical innovation rather than seeing it as an attempt to escape charges of theoretical inconsistency, and that will be because they refuse to read Žižek politically and, instead, think that their duty is to follow him.

25

On Žižek's Dialectics

Vighi, F. (2012) *On Žižek's Dialectics: Surplus, Subtraction, Sublimation.* London: Continuum.

Every reading of Slavoj Žižek, including those undertaken by the master himself of his own earlier writings, is a rereading, a reconstruction of lines of argument that have become snagged by the incompatible sharply-honed intricacies of Lacanian psychoanalysis and Marxism and their resistance to his insistent conceptual reduction of them to German idealism. The worst of that reduction surfaces from time to time in Fabio Vighi's discussion of the way Žižek 'engages with Christianity in order to solicit from its narrative a revolutionary dialectic' (p. 131), but it functions throughout this otherwise excellent book as a subterranean assumption that it is '*the vertiginous dimension of thought itself*' (p. 142) that is the stuff of an 'act', an 'event' and of the very 'political parallax' through which we might redeem ourselves as we overthrow capitalism. There is good discussion of the limitations of adjacent political traditions, which include Hardt and Negri, Karatani and Badiou, but the epithet 'idealist' is used as a term of abuse, which is a bit rich coming from a perspective that eschews any actual grounding in the material struggles that threaten to revolutionise the means of production.

Despite, or perhaps because of, the contradictory matrix that Žižek has formed as a reflective apparatus to grasp the nature of a no less contradictory political-economic system, Vighi constructs a faithful reading of the place of dialectics that also inches forward toward a political perspective that, as it were, 'thinks' its way beyond 'the massive task of thinking' (p. 142) that Žižek is most-times trapped within. This is, as Vighi reminds us, a tricky task because there is no direct link between Lacanian psychoanalysis and democratic politics, or any particular politics as such. Here he pits himself against some of the leftish enthusiasts for psychoanalysis who then attempt to find in the framework an implicit warrant for some form of 'democratic' vision of society. Such an attempt is implausible enough when confined to Freud, but quite impossible when Lacan is brought into the equation. There are acute comments about the importance of 'negativity' which run as a thread through this breathtakingly lucid account of Žižek's work. And, apart from rehearsing the importance of 'dialectics', there are carefully crafted connections between dialectics and the homologous relationship between Marx and Freud.

The mainspring for this endeavour is the connection between Marx's specification of 'surplus value' (extracted by the employer from the surplus labour carried out by the worker) and Lacan's 'surplus jouissance' (excessive enjoyment that is domesticated under capitalism as marketable packets of pleasure). Marcuse – another very suitable link back to Hegel from psychoanalysis – is evoked at key points in the text to show how the worker has been thoroughly incorporated into the system, and other revolutionary agents are summoned to help us out of this predicament, such as slum-dwellers (p. 21) or the figure of the child (p. 46).

The problem with this, and it connects with the problem of 'idealism' (and indeed the claim made in the book that Žižek really provides a 'dialectical materialist' alternative), is that there is a curious reframing of past historical struggles against exploitation as if they were at root expressions of what Marcuse called 'the Great Refusal' (p. 128), rather than (alongside calls for 'freedom', which is easier to incorporate into an idealist problematic) quite concrete demands for, say, 'bread' and 'peace'. The revolutionary Marxist task of constructing alternative forms of society in opposition to the old forms culminating in 'dual power' (in which the revolutionary forces provide a pole of attraction to break the capitalist state and thus build something better) is completely absent from the circuit of conceptual puzzles this book confines itself to. This might be what Vighi is hinting at though when he calls for 'an audacious creative socio-political project whose consistency is equal to, and materializes, the Real limit of theory itself' (p. 153).

There are moments, all too few moments, when Vighi is forced to contemplate some possible limitations in Žižek's work; that there is a risk of privileging 'an abstract Real' (p. 111) and that his injunction to 'do nothing' is actually not very dialectical at all (p. 138). This rather muted critique, which is effectively also in the frame of the book a self-critique, could be taken further, and it certainly needs to be turned around upon psychoanalysis, which functions here as a code-breaking mechanism that will lay bare the contradictions of capitalism. The whole point of the 'act', Vighi argues, 'is that *this gesture should be applied to theory itself*' (p. 112), so would it also be possible to treat psychoanalysis itself as part of the problem rather than as the solution? Rather than assuming that psychoanalysis provides the master key to unlock the mysteries of 'surplus jouissance' in which 'surplus value' is grounded (which is the way Vighi presents the relationship between the two, in an account that privileges psychoanalysis over Marxism), should we not examine how the 'lock' itself is constructed such that psychoanalysis appears to be the only key that will fit it and so confirm its apparently immutable universal structure?

Many of the contradictions in this sympathetic reconstruction of the role of dialectics in Žižek's work are apparent precisely because Vighi has set the terms of the argument so clearly, and he then makes it possible for the reader to register the importance of fruitful conceptual connections (and one or two worrying elisions) and mark their own critical distance from the text. Such distance may not be an expression of 'absolute spontaneity and pure, unendurable imagination' (p. 164), and neither will it thereby accord with an Ur-psychoanalytic vision of Hegelian freedom. Instead it is Vighi himself who, in this surprisingly accessible and enjoyable book, sets the conditions for us to work with it dialectically and perhaps come closer to the political project he aims for.

References

Barthes, R. (1982) *Empire of Signs* (translated by R. Howard). New York: Hill and Wang.

Bensaïd, D. (2002) *Marx for Our Times: Adventures and Misadventures of a Critique*. London: Verso.

Bhaskar, R. (1989) *Reclaiming Reality: A Critical Introduction to Contemporary Philosophy*. London: Verso.

Biko, S. (1978) *I Write What I Like*. London: Bowerdean.

Billig, M. (1999) *Freudian Repression: Conversation Creating the Unconscious*. Cambridge: Cambridge University Press.

Birksted-Breen, D., Flanders, S. and Gibeault, A. (eds.) (2010) *Reading French Psychoanalysis*. London: Routledge.

Blowers, GH and Yang, SH (1997) 'Freud's *Deshi*: The coming of psychoanalysis to Japan', *Journal of the History of the Behavioral Sciences*, 33 (2): 115–126.

Blowers, GH and Yang, SH (2001) 'Ohtsuki Kenji and the beginnings of lay analysis in Japan', *International Journal of Psychoanalysis*, 82 (27): 27–42.

Brannen, N. (1991) *The Practical English-Japanese Dictionary*. New York and Tokyo: Weatherhill Inc.

Brown, SD and Stenner, P. (2009) *Psychology without Foundations: History, Philosophy and Psychosocial Theory*. London: Sage.

Buruma, I. (1995) *A Japanese Mirror: Heroes and Villains of Japanese Culture*. London: Vintage.

Chakrabarti, A. and Dhar, A. (2010) *Dislocation and Resettlement in Development: From Third World to the World of the Third*. London and New York: Routledge.

Clough, PT with Halley, J. (eds.) (2007) *The Affective Turn: Theorizing the Social*. Durham, NC: Duke University Press.

Danziger, K. (1990) *Constructing the Subject: Historical Origins of Psychological Research*. Cambridge: Cambridge University Press.

De Vos, J. (2011) 'Psychologization or the discontents of psycho-analysis', *Psychoanalysis, Culture & Society*, 16, 354–372.

De Vos, J. (2012) *Psychologisation in Times of Globalisation*. London: Routledge.

Dean, J. (2006) *Žižek's Politics*. London and New York: Routledge.

Doi, T. (1973) *The Anatomy of Dependence* (translated by J. Bester). Tokyo: Kodansha International.

Dufour, D-R (2008) *The Art of Shrinking Heads: On the New Servitude of the Liberated in the Age of Total Capitalism*. Cambridge: Polity Press.

Dunker, CIL (2011) *The Constitution of the Psychoanalytic Clinic: A History of Its Structure and Power*. London: Karnac.

Easthope, A. (1999) *Englishness and National Culture*. London: Routledge.

Endo, F. (2002) 'Kojin Karatani and The Return of the Thirties: Psychoanalysis in/of Japan', *The Semiotic Review of Books*, 13 (1), www.chass.utoronto.ca/epc/srb/srb/kojin.pdf (accessed 22 January 04).

Enriquez, V. (1994) *From Colonial to Liberation Psychology: The Philippine Experience (2nd Edition)*. Manila: De La Salle University Press.

Fanon, F. (1967) *Black Skin, White Masks*. New York: Grove Press.

Fink, B. (1995) *The Lacanian Subject: Between Language and Jouissance*. Princeton, New Jersey: Princeton University Press.

Fink, B. (1999) *A Clinical Introduction to Lacanian Psychoanalysis: Theory and Technique*. Cambridge, MA: Harvard University Press.

Foucault, M. (1977) *Language, Counter-Memory, Practice: Selected Essays and Interviews*. Oxford: Blackwell.

Foucault, M. (2003) In Bertani, M. and Fontana, A. (eds.) *Society Must be Defended: Lectures at the Collège de France, 1975–1976*. London: Allen Lane.

Freud, S. (1913 [1912–1913]) 'Totem and taboo', in S. Freud (1966–1974) *The Standard Edition of the Complete Psychological*

Works of Sigmund Freud (translated by J. Strachey). London: Vintage, Hogarth Press and the Institute of Psycho-Analysis, vol. XIII.

Freud, S. (1933) 'New Introductory Lectures on Psychoanalysis', in S. Freud (1966–1974) *The Standard Edition of the Complete Psychological Works of Sigmund Freud* (translated by J. Strachey). London: Vintage, Hogarth Press and the Institute of Psycho-Analysis, vol. XXII.

Frosh, S. (2010) *Psychoanalysis Outside the Clinic: Interventions in Psychosocial Studies*. London: Palgrave Macmillan.

Gergen, KJ (1991) *The Saturated Self: Dilemmas of Identity in Contemporary Life*. New York: Basic Books.

Gherovici, P. and Steinkoler, M. (eds.) (2015) *Lacan on Madness: Madness, Yes You Can't*. London and New York: Routledge.

Gilligan, C. (1982) *In a Different Voice: Psychological Theory and Women's Development*. Harvard: MIT Press.

Golan, R. (2006) *Loving Psychoanalysis: Looking at Culture with Freud and Lacan*. London: Karnac.

Gordo, A. and De Vos, J. (eds.) (2010) 'Psychologisation under Scrutiny' (special issue), *Annual Review of Critical Psychology*, 8.

Holzkamp, K. (1992) 'On doing psychology critically', in I. Parker (ed.) (2011) *Critical Psychology: Critical Concepts in Psychology, Volume 4, Alternatives and Visions for Change*. London and New York: Routledge.

Hook, D. (2007) *Foucault, Psychology and the Analytics of Power*. Basingstoke: Palgrave Macmillan.

Hook, D. (2012) *A Critical Psychology of the Postcolonial: The Mind of Apartheid*. London and New York: Routledge.

House, R. and Totton, N. (eds.) (1997) *Implausible Professions: Arguments for Pluralism and Autonomy in Psychotherapy and Counselling*. Ross-on-Wye: PCCS.

Ichiyo, M. (1987) *Class Struggle and Technological Innovation in Japan since 1945*. Amsterdam: IIRE.

Jaynes, J. (1976) *The Origins of Consciousness in the Breakdown of the*

Bicameral Mind. Boston: Houghton-Mifflin.

Jerry, PA (1998) 'The Brief Lacanian Therapy (BLT) Project'. http://www3.memlane.com/pajerry/lacan.htm

Kotsko, A. (2008) *Žižek and Theology*. London: Continuum.

Lacan, J. (1971) *The Seminar. Book XVIII: On a discourse that might not be a semblance* (translated from unedited French manuscripts by C. Gallagher), unpublished.

Lacan, J. (1988) 'Logical Time and the Assertion of Anticipated Certainty: A New Sophism' (translated by B. Fink and M. Silver), *Newsletter of the Freudian Field*, 2, pp. 4–22.

Lacan, J. (1991/2007) *The Other Side of Psychoanalysis: The Seminar of Jacques Lacan, Book XVII*. New York: WW Norton and Co.

Lacan, J. (1975/1998) *On Feminine Sexuality, The Limits of Love and Knowledge, 1972–1973: Encore, The Seminar of Jacques Lacan, Book XX* (translated by B. Fink). New York: Norton.

Lacan, J. (2001) 'Avis au lecteur japonais', in *Autres Écrits*, J-A Miller (ed.). Paris: du Seuil, pp. 497–499.

Laqueur, T. (2003) *Solitary Sex: A Cultural History of Masturbation*. New York: Zone.

Loose, R. (2002) *The Subject of Addiction: Psychoanalysis and the Administration of Enjoyment*. London and New York: Karnac Books.

Mamdani, M. (2004) 'Race and ethnicity as political identities in the African context', in N. Tazi (ed.) *Keywords, Identity: For a Different Kind of Globalization*. New Delhi: Vistaar.

Mandel, E. (1984) *Delightful Murder: A Social History of the Crime Story*. London: Pluto Press.

Manganyi, NC (1973) *Being-Black-in-the-World*. Johannesburg: Ravan Press.

Manning, P. (2005) *Freud and American Sociology*. Cambridge: Polity.

Mannoni, O. (1964) *Prospero and Caliban: The Psychology of Colonization (2nd Edition)*. New York: Praeger.

Martín-Baró, I. (1994) *Writings for a Liberation Psychology*.

Cambridge, MA: Harvard University Press.

Miller, J-A (1999) 'Interpretation in Reverse', *Psychoanalytical Notebooks of the London Circle*, 2: 9–18.

Miller, J-A (2002) 'Elements of epistemology', in J. Glynos and Y. Stavrakakis (eds.) *Lacan and Science*. London: Karnac.

Miller, J-A (2008) 'Clinic under transference', *Psychoanalytical Notebooks*, 17: 7–12.

Moloney, JC (1953) 'Understanding the Paradox of Japanese Psychoanalysis', *International Journal of Psycho-Analysis*, 34 (4): 291–303.

Mowbray, R. (1995) *The Case Against Psychotherapy Registration: A Conservation Issue for the Human Potential Movement*. London: Trans Marginal Press.

Nobus, D. (2002) 'Illiterature', in L. Thurston (ed.) *Re-inventing the Symptom: Essays on the Final Lacan*. New York: Other Press, pp. 19–43.

Okonogi, K. (1995) 'Japan', in P. Kutter (ed.) *Psychoanalysis International: A Guide to Psychoanalysis Throughout the World Volume 2*. Stuttgart-Bad-Cannstatt: Frommann-Holzboog, pp. 123–141.

Oyama, T., Sato, T. and Suzuki, Y. (2001) 'Shaping of scientific psychology in Japan', *International Journal of Psychology*, 36 (6), pp. 396–406.

Pound, M. (2007) *Theology, Psychoanalysis and Trauma*. London: SCM Press.

Pound, M. (2008) *Žižek: A (Very) Critical Introduction*. Grand Rapids, MI: Eerdmans Publishing Co.

Richards, G. (1996) *Putting Psychology in its Place: An Introduction from a Critical Historical Perspective*. London: Routledge.

Richards, G. (2012) *'Race', Racism and Psychology: Towards a Reflexive History (2nd Edition)*. London and New York: Routledge.

Rose, N. (1985) *The Psychological Complex: Psychology, Politics and Society in England 1869–1939*. London: Routledge and Kegan

Paul.

Shingu, K. (2004) *Being Irrational: Lacan, the Objet a, and the Golden Mean* (translated and edited by Michael Radich).Tokyo: Gakuju Shoin.

Sohn-Rethel, A. (1978) *Intellectual and Manual Labour: A Critique of Epistemology*. London: Macmillan.

Stavrakakis, Y. (2007) *The Lacanian Left*. Edinburgh: Edinburgh University Press.

Terre Blanche, M. and Durrheim, K. (eds.) (1999) *Research in Practice: Applied Methods for the Social Sciences*. Cape Town: UCT Press.

Totton, N. (ed.) (2006) *The Politics of Psychotherapy: New Perspectives*. Buckingham: Open University Press.

Vanheule, S. (2011) *The Subject of Psychosis: A Lacanian Perspective*. London: Palgrave Macmillan.

Vighi, F. (2012) *On Žižek's Dialectics: Surplus, Subtraction, Sublimation*. London: Continuum.

Voruz, V. (2007) 'A Lacanian reading of *Dora*'. In: V. Voruz and B. Wolf (eds.) *The Later Lacan: An Introduction*. New York: State University of New York Press, pp. 158–179.

Žižek, S. (1989) *The Sublime Object of Ideology*. London: Verso.

Žižek, S. (2006) *The Parallax View*. Cambridge, MA: MIT Press.

Žižek, S. (2008) *Violence: Six Sideways Reflections*. London: Profile Books.

Zero Books
CULTURE, SOCIETY & POLITICS

Contemporary culture has eliminated the concept and public figure of
the intellectual. A cretinous anti-intellectualism presides, cheer-led by
hacks in the pay of multinational corporations who reassure their
bored readers that there is no need to rouse themselves from their
stupor. Zer0 Books knows that another kind of discourse - intellectual
without being academic, popular without being populist - is not only
possible: it is already flourishing. Zer0 is convinced that in the
unthinking, blandly consensual culture in which we live, critical and
engaged theoretical reflection is more important than ever before.

If you have enjoyed this book, why not tell other readers by
posting a review on your preferred book site. Recent bestsellers from
Zero Books are:

In the Dust of This Planet
Horror of Philosophy vol. 1
Eugene Thacker

In the first of a series of three books on the Horror of
Philosophy, *In the Dust of This Planet* offers the genre of horror
as a way of thinking about the unthinkable.
Paperback: 978-1-84694-676-9 ebook: 978-1-78099-010-1

Capitalist Realism
Is there no alternative?
Mark Fisher

An analysis of the ways in which capitalism has presented itself
as the only realistic political-economic system.
Paperback: 978-1-84694-317-1 ebook: 978-1-78099-734-6

Rebel Rebel
Chris O'Leary
David Bowie: every single song. Everything you want to know, everything you didn't know.
Paperback: 978-1-78099-244-0 ebook: 978-1-78099-713-1

Cartographies of the Absolute
Alberto Toscano, Jeff Kinkle
An aesthetics of the economy for the twenty-first century.
Paperback: 978-1-78099-275-4 ebook: 978-1-78279-973-3

Malign Velocities
Accelerationism and Capitalism
Benjamin Noys
Longlisted for the Bread and Roses Prize 2015, *Malign Velocities* argues against the need for speed, tracking acceleration as the symptom of the ongoing crises of capitalism.
Paperback: 978-1-78279-300-7 ebook: 978-1-78279-299-4

Readers of ebooks can buy or view any of these bestsellers by clicking on the live link in the title. Most titles are published in paperback and as an ebook. Paperbacks are available in traditional bookshops. Both print and ebook formats are available online.

Find more titles and sign up to our readers' newsletter at
http://www.johnhuntpublishing.com/culture-and-politics
Follow us on Facebook at https://www.facebook.com/ZeroBooks
and Twitter at https://twitter.com/Zer0Books